Taking the NREMT test or State EMT exam can be a painless experie
knowledge of the course material AND an understanding of what to ex
created this page to aid in answering some of the more common questi
state EMT certification tests. This includes facts and advice related to t
intended to aid the EMT candidate in his or her pursuit of certification and registration as an EMT, ~~~~~,
Paramedic.

Many states have adopted the NREMT cognitive exam as their state exam, however there are a few states that still hold their own exam. The information given here is more specific for the NREMT Computer Adaptive Test (CAT), however the test taking tips are useful for any exam. If you are not going to be taking the NREMT exam, you should contact the state EMS office where you will be testing and see if they provide a study guide for their exam. These study guides are very useful for state specific exams.

Over the years the NREMT exam format has changed from a linear exam (paper and pencil) to the CAT exam. This is an adaptive exam and will vary in length. It is not graded like a traditional linear exam.

Facts That You Need To Know About The NREMT Exam

- NREMT test questions are multiple choice with 4 potential answers. A committee of 10-20 EMS experts, who must all agree that the question is in line with the most current practice analysis study, creates all questions. These EMS experts make sure that there is only one "best" or "correct" answer, and that "each incorrect answer has some level of plausibility." Additionally, each question and answer must be easily found in common text books used in teaching EMS classes.

- As of January 1, 2007 the NREMT has changed its exam formatting to a CBT (Computer Based Testing) method. Exams will no longer be delivered via a paper test and completed with a pencil. All testing will be performed at a computer workstation. PearsonVue testing centers all over the United States administer these tests.

- The CBT that the NREMT is now utilizing is called CAT or (Computer Adaptive Testing) and each exam is tailored specifically to the individual EMT candidate. This testing method is considered state of the art and uses a theory called IRT (Item Response Theory). IRT is a statistical way to measure a person's ability based on the fact that the probability of a person answering a question correctly is directly related to their ability and the difficulty level of the question. Combining CAT with IRT should make NREMT exams more precise, fair, and accurate. What does that mean? Basically each item (question) is given a weighted point value. This value is based on the difficulty of the question. A harder question has a higher point value. An easier question has a lower value.

- New CAT NREMT tests will deliver questions one at a time to the candidate and will NOT be randomly chosen. They are rated along the same ability scale as the candidate is exhibiting proficiency. The first questions on the exam are generally just below the passing standard. If a question is asked that is below the candidate's level of ability, the probability is high for the candidate to answer the question correctly. If a question asked is above a candidate's level of ability, they have a high probability of missing it. If the candidate answers the question correctly then a slightly more difficult question will be delivered next. As the difficulty of the questions increase, eventually the candidate will start to miss questions. The questions then become slightly easier and the candidate will begin to answer correctly again. At this point in the exam the application algorithm calculates an ability estimate for this candidate and begins delivering questions that are slightly harder and slightly easier than the candidate's ability. As the CAT exam progresses, the ability estimate gets more and more precise as the pattern of right to wrong answers stabilizes around the client's true ability. The exam will end at the point when there is a 95% certainty that the candidate's true ability is above or below the passing standard. It can also end if you run out of questions or time, however both of these instances are rare.

- CAT and IRT match the question difficulty to the candidate's perceived level of ability, this limits the number of questions delivered as well as increases accuracy.

- Exam fees can be paid online at the NREMT website, but you must first be registered and sign into your account. You can pay by credit card, or with a payment voucher if your school provides one. You may also mail in payment, however this will delay your ability to schedule your exam until the payment has cleared.

- If you do not pass the exam you may retake it after 14 days. This period is to provide you with time to study.

- NREMT test results are generally available within 1 to 2 business days on the NREMT website. Check your exam results here www.nremt.org

Advice On How To Take And Pass The NREMT Exam And State EMT Tests

This advice has been gleaned from dozens of sources. Information contained here has been compiled from interviews with EMTs and Paramedics who have taken and passed the tests multiple times. It has also been gathered from EMS related discussion forums and nationally recognized test-taking authorities.

What Material To Study For The NREMT Exam

- Technically, you should know everything that was covered in the EMT course materials. There aren't any secret methods or insights that can replace proper test preparation, but some things are common. The tests are heavy in the basics. Know CPR and shock as well as all of the segment categories of the test itself i.e. Airway, Ventilation and Oxygenation; Trauma; Cardiology; Medical; and Operations. Know the major components of the airway and the normal ranges of respiration for adults and pediatric patients. Know diabetic emergencies and the various causes of syncope. You will see about 15% of your questions related to pediatrics, and about 85% related to adults. These will be spread out through the 5 categories listed above.

- A large portion of the exam is related to operations and many students overlook this. Since September 11, 2001 a great effort has been made to incorporate more education about NIMS and ICS with regard to EMS. Understand how these systems work and how they apply to a mass casualty and you will be a step ahead of other candidates.

- The NREMT exam is NOT based upon the textbook you used in your class. The exam is based upon the NREMT Practice Analysis done every five years. The exam questions are written to fall within the Department of Transportation EMT Curriculum. EMT textbooks only give you their interpretation of those standards. (NOTE: The new National EMS Education Standards are EMR (Emergency Medical Responder), EMT, AEMT (Advanced EMT), and Paramedic.)

- Remember, although the NREMT exam looks for a minimum entry-level competency, nobody wants a "just made it by the skin of their teeth" partner. Know your stuff. The more knowledge you have about EMS, the shorter your test will be. If you are answering questions well above the competency line, your exam will end closer to the minimum number of questions rather than the maximum number of questions.

- Obviously take advantage of the EMT and Paramedic Practice Tests here in this book and on the website. There is detailed score tracking and exam review features that let you see your strong and weak areas while you continue to take exams and improve. Identify your strong and weak areas so you can study to improve all around. Use online information resources like Wikipedia to help broaden your subject knowledge and branch out from the knowledge of a single textbook.

Before Taking The NREMT Exam Or State Test

- Eat a well balanced diet and drink plenty of water the day before. Include B vitamin foods like bananas, oatmeal, and raisins, and get plenty of rest. Reschedule if you are sick. Don't attempt the test if you aren't feeling your best.

- Don't cram! If you don't know it the night before the test, you will most likely not know it for the test. Relax or sleep instead of cramming.

- Don't consume a bunch of coffee or sugar before the exam it will only make your anxiety worse. Studies show that consuming caffeine and/or sugar actually slows your brain down and results in lower grades on exams.

- Study regularly for a few weeks before you test. Use the resources from this website, and any other resources you might have to study. Identify your weak areas and then focus your learning in those areas. If possible, you should study for a couple of weeks after completing your EMS course, and then test. Don't wait a long time if you have the ability to test sooner.

- Know exactly where the test center is and arrive early to eliminate the stress of being late. Remember, you have to be signed up for the test. You cannot just walk in and take it. Bring your photo ID and a couple of pencils. Scrap paper will be provided for you and it must be turned in with your exam.

- When you go to take the test dress in multiple layers so that you can shed what you do not need and still be comfortable. Temperatures of testing centers can vary a great deal throughout the day especially if it is a rarely used room or building. Being nervous will cause your vessels to constrict and you will feel colder than you might normally feel. Shivering during a test is no fun!

- Go to the bathroom before the test. You are allowed to go during the exam, but take care of it sooner rather than later. If you have to leave the testing room you will be required to take one form of ID with you while the other stays within the testing center, and it will be verified each time you leave and enter.

- You must bring two forms of ID to the exam site, and at least one of them must have a photo ID.

During The NREMT Exam Or State Test

- You CANNOT skip a question and come back to it later. The nature of the CAT exam requires that you answer each question individually before any additional questions are delivered. The next question you get delivered is based on how you answered the previous questions. This is why you must make a choice before you can proceed.

- Look out for words like EXCEPT, ALWAYS, NEVER, MOST APPROPRIATE and other qualifiers. Anything that puts limits on the potential answer should be a flag to slow down and read the question and all answers very carefully.

- Read the whole question thoroughly at least a couple of times and formulate the answer in your head BEFORE you look at the answer choices. If you look at the answer choices prior to understanding the question completely, you can be lead to choose an incorrect answer. The test is timed, but by slowing down, you will actually have a shorter test. Don't worry about the time, worry about making the correct choice.

- For each question there are 4 potential answers. All of the choices must have some plausibility to them. It is possible that all 4 choices are correct, or that all 4 choices are wrong. You must choose the "most" correct choice available, even if it is not what you would normally do first.

- Do not complicate the scenario or situation. Do not bring elements into the questions that are not there. This will cause you to overlook the basics, which is probably what the question is testing for.

- Relax, and remember to breath adequately. Slow deep your breath by breathing in through your nose, and then exhaling out through your mouth. Repeat. Do this as often as you find yourself hurrying, rushing, or getting angry.

The NREMT's Newest Test Plan

The National Registry test plan changed on September 1, 2010. The new test plan now covers five topic areas: Airway, Ventilation and Oxygenation; Trauma; Cardiology; Medical and Operations. This plan applies to all national EMS certification levels.

A total of 85% of the exam items cover adult patients and 15% cover pediatric patients. Former items that covered OB are now part of the medical section of the exam. Examinations are not scored on the basis of topic areas (sections). Passing an examination still requires successful demonstration of entry-level competency over the entire domain of the test.

The changes in the test plan are the result of an NREMT research project that prioritized tasks all EMS providers accomplish while providing care. The NREMT test plan is designed to cover the important tasks of the job. The NREMT Board adopted this plan in November of 2009. Items in the test bank are the same items that were in previous test banks. The emphasis is just different because the NREMT adjusted the emphasis of the test based upon EMS provider data.

The NREMT EMR Exam

Has between 80 and 110 questions. You have 1 hour and 45 minutes to complete the exam. Cost of the NREMT EMR Exam is $65.00. The exam will cover the entire spectrum of EMS care including: Airway, Ventilation, Oxygenation; Trauma; Cardiology; Medical; and EMS Operations. Items related to patient care are focused on adult patients (85%) and pediatric patients (15%). In order to pass the exam, you must meet a standard level of competency. The passing standard is defined by the ability to provide safe and effective entry-level emergency medical care.

The NREMT EMT Exam

Has between 70 and 120 questions. You have two hours to complete the test. Cost of the NREMT Exam is $70.00. The exam will cover the entire spectrum of EMS care including: Airway, Ventilation, Oxygenation; Trauma; Cardiology; Medical; and EMS Operations. Items related to patient care are focused on adult patients (85%) and pediatric patients (15%). In order to pass the exam, you must meet a standard level of competency. The passing standard is defined by the ability to provide safe and effective entry-level emergency medical care.

The NREMT AEMT Exam

Is a Computer Based Test (CBT). There are 135 questions that each candidate must answer in 2 hours and 15 minutes. The exam will cover the entire spectrum of EMS care including: Airway, Respiration & Ventilation; Cardiology & Resuscitation; Trauma; Medical & Obstetrics/Gynecology; and EMS Operations. Items related to patient care are focused on adult and geriatric patients (85%) and pediatric patients (15%). In order to pass the exam, you must meet a standard level of competency. The passing standard is defined by the ability to provide safe and effective entry -level advanced emergency medical care.

The NREMT EMT Paramedic Exam

Has between 80 and 150 questions and you have 2 hours and 30 minutes to complete the exam. Cost of the NREMT Paramedic Exam is $110.00. The exam will cover the entire spectrum of EMS care including: Airway, Ventilation, Oxygenation; Trauma; Cardiology; Medical; and EMS Operations. Items related to patient care are focused on adult patients (85%) and pediatric patients (15%). In order to pass the exam, you must meet a standard level of competency. The passing standard is defined by the ability to provide safe and effective entry-level emergency medical care.

How NREMT Exams and Questions are Constructed

Most of the National Exams given in the United States follow the formula below in developing questions. The NREMT is one of these tests. If you start to understand what type of questions you are being asked, it will allow you to begin to know how to apply the correct response. This is some deep reading, but has helped many people in their test taking. Read through the information, and then see if you can start to figure it out as you take practice tests. We will try to give a few examples at the end.

In 1956, Benjamin Bloom headed a group of educational psychologists who developed a classification of levels of intellectual behavior important in learning. Bloom found that over 95% of the test questions students encountered required them to think only at the lowest possible level...the recall of information.

Bloom identified six levels within the cognitive domain, from the simple recall or recognition of facts as the lowest level, through increasingly more complex and abstract mental levels, to the highest order, which is classified as evaluation. Verb examples that represent intellectual activity on each level are listed here.

1. Knowledge: arrange, define, duplicate, label, list, memorize, name, order, recognize, relate, recall, repeat, reproduce, state.

2. Comprehension: classify, describe, discuss, explain, express, identify, indicate, locate, recognize, report, restate, review, select, translate.

3. Application: apply, choose, demonstrate, dramatize, employ, illustrate, interpret, operate, practice, schedule, sketch, solve, use, write.

4. Analysis: analyze, appraise, calculate, categorize, compare, contrast, criticize, differentiate, discriminate, distinguish, examine, experiment, question, test.

5. Synthesis: arrange, assemble, collect, compose, construct, create, design, develop, formulate, manage, organize, plan, prepare, propose, set up, write.

6. Evaluation: appraise, argue, assess, attach, choose, compare, defend, estimate, judge, predict, rate, core, select, support, value, evaluate.

The chart below shows the increasing level of complexity of question construction.

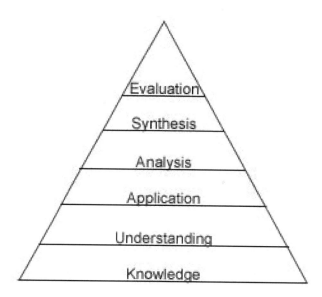

The NREMT exam follows a similar formula in that it starts with the basic Knowledge then begins to increase the style of question to determine the candidate's true grasp of a subject. This is why you will see similar questions during the test. Questions will be written in a slightly different way to see if you truly grasp the concept around it.

Questions given during your training are questions in the "knowledge" category 80% to 90% of the time. These questions are not bad, but using them all the time is. Instructors should try to utilize higher order level of questions. These questions require much more "brain power" and a more extensive and elaborate answer. Below are the six question categories as defined by Bloom. After each one is an example of how the question would be worded (started) so that you can begin to decipher at what level this question is being formed.

KNOWLEDGE
- Remembering;
- Memorizing;
- Recognizing;
- Recalling identification
- Recall of information
  ○ Who, what, when, where, how ...?
  ○ Describe

COMPREHENSION
- Interpreting;
- Translating from one medium to another;
- Describing in one's own words;
- Organization and selection of facts and ideas
  ○ Retell...

APPLICATION
- Problem solving;
- Applying information to produce some result;
- Use of facts, rules, and principles;
  ○ How is...an example of ...?
  ○ How is...related to ...?
  ○ Why is...significant?

ANALYSIS

- Subdividing something to show how it is put together;
- Finding the underlying structure of a communication;
- Identifying motives;
- Separation of a whole into component parts;
  - What are the parts or features of ...?
  - Classify...according to...
  - Outline/Diagram...
  - How does...compare/contrast with...?
  - What evidence can you list ...?

SYNTHESIS

- Creating a unique, original product that may be in verbal form or may be a physical object;
- Combination of ideas to form a new whole;
  - What would you predict/infer from...?
  - What ideas can you add to...?
  - How would you create/design a new...?
  - What might happen if you combined...?
  - What solutions would you suggest for...?

EVALUATION

- Making value decisions about issues;
- Resolving controversies or differences of opinion;
- Development of opinions, judgments, or decisions
  - Do you agree...?
  - What do you think about...?
  - What is the most important...?
  - Place the following in order of priority...
  - How would you decide about...?
  - What criteria would you use to assess...?

This is the nuts and bolts of how an NREMT exam is built. Below is an example of how an NREMT question is constructed. This will give you some insight into the thinking behind each question.

Steps to Question Writing

A well-designed multiple-choice item consists of three main components: a stem (asks a question or poses a statement which requires completion), key (the correct answer/s), and distracter(s) (incorrect option/s). The following section is designed to enhance the candidate's understanding of the NREMT question writing process.

Step 1. Select an area of the test plan for the focus of the item.
* Patient Assessment

Step 2. Select a subcategory from the chosen area of the test plan.
* Multiple patient incidents

Step 3. Select an important concept within that subcategory.
* Assess and triage among a group of patients to prioritize the order of care delivery

Step 4. Use the concept selected and write the stem.
* The EMT arrives on scene of a vehicle accident.
Which is the most critical patient that should be transported first?

Step 5. Write a key to represent important information the entry-level EMT should know.
* Altered Level of Consciousness
~ A patient who doesn't remember the accident or what the day is

Step 6. Identify common errors, misconceptions, or irrelevant information.
* Distracting injuries
* Smell of alcohol
* Lack of understanding of expected findings related to a specific clinical finding

Step 7. Use the previous information and write the distracters
~ A patient who has a large bleeding gash to the right arm
~ A patient who smells of alcohol and is having trouble walking
~ A patient with moderate Alzheimer's disease (AD) who is asking to talk with the spouse who died several years ago

Step 8. Complete the item using the stem, key, and distracters.
The EMT arrives on scene of a multiple vehicle accident. After assuring scene safety and assessing the patients, whom should the EMT transport first?
1. The patient who doesn't remember the accident or what day it is. (Key)
2. The patient with a large bleeding gash to the right arm.
3. The patient who smells like alcohol and is having trouble walking straight.
4. The patient, whose family states, has moderate Alzheimer's disease and is asking to talk to a spouse who died several years ago.

In this example you can see that the question is asked at the Evaluation level of Bloom's Taxonomy. That is the highest form of question. It requires you to know information about each answer option, and then weigh each against the other to determine an order of care. In this sample question you can see that a patient with an altered level of consciousness would be the most critical given the information you have. A large bleeding gash is a distracting injury, easily treated with bandaging, and not requiring the most immediate transport. A patient who smells like alcohol and is possibly intoxicated does not in itself warrant immediate transport. This would probably be the second most critical due to mechanism and not being able to determine LOC as easily as others. The patient who is asking to speak to a dead spouse has a disease that would make this type of response normal. This is the type of question that the NREMT likes to give. It requires you to really think about each option and only use the information presented in the question and answers.

Question 1: You are dispatched to an amusement park where a 16-month-old boy is reported to have something wedged in his throat. Dispatch says that the child is breathing, but it sounds very noisy like a whistle. Upon arrival you can see that the child is breathing with stridor, is pale, and is beginning to turn blue around the lips. What is the best treatment plan for this patient?

a. Try to see the object in the child's throat and remove with your fingers if possible. Call for additional help if unable to remove the object.

b. Give the child 3 back slaps and 3 abdominal thrusts. If the object does not dislodge, begin transport with non-reabreather mask and O2.

c. Begin transport while giving blow-by oxygen. Continue to monitor the status of the child's airway en route to the hospital.

d. Perform pediatric Heimlich thrusts with an upward motion slightly lower than those used on adults.

Question 2: You arrive on scene with your partner Stuart to a multi-car collision involving at least 6 patients. You have called for additional units to help you out with the scene. What should you do next?

a. Perform a detailed history on the patients

b. Begin treating the patients immediately

c. Prioritize and triage the patients

d. Check to see who the youngest is and treat them

Question 3: You and your partner Bob are called to the scene of a man down. The report said the man has no pulse and that family members are doing CPR. Upon arriving at the scene what 3 things are you going to do first?

a. Open their airway, tell the bystander to stop CPR, and put your gloves on

b. Question the bystanders, direct them to stop CPR ,and check for pulse

c. Hook up the AED, open their airway, and insert an adjunct

d. Attach the AED, tell everyone to stand back, and hit the analyze button

Question 4: Dispatch has reported that there is a man passed out behind a supermarket and he is not breathing. You arrive to find a male sitting alone up against a wall. His eyes are closed and he does not respond to your attempts to elicit an answer. He is breathing at 8 irregular breaths per minute with periods of apnea. There is a baggy with a white substance on the ground next to him. When you give him a sternal rub, he grabs his chest with his hand, but does not make any noise. What is this man's GCS and what is the best course of action?

a. GCS of 7 / Assist ventilation via BVM

b. GCS of 7 / Restrain the man to the gurney with the likelihood of drug ingestion

c. GCS of 6 / Put him on high flow O2 via NRB and transport

d. GCS of 6 / Insert a nasopharyngeal and prepare to suction

Question 5: You are called to the scene of a man down. Dispatch reports the man is pulseless and bystanders are doing CPR. According to the NREMT Cardiac Arrest Management/AED skill sheet, which of the following sequences is appropriate?

a. Check for responsiveness, Assess for breathing, Check carotid pulse , put your gloves on

b. Question the bystanders, direct them to stop CPR , check for pulse and then attach the AED, Begin chest compressions

c. Turn on power to AED, open the patient's airway, insert an adjunct and then analyze the rhythm

d. Complete one cycle of CPR, Attach the AED, Have everyone stand clear during rhythm check

Question 6: You arrive on scene for a possible poisoning. The patient is a 9 month old girl who was found with an open bottle of drain cleaner. She has a bump on her forehead and is noticeably irritable. During your assessment you note that the child does not make eye contact with you at all. Which of the following is the best course of action and why?

a. Initiate transport with blow by oxygen. The lack of eye contact and irritability are concerning signs in children this age.
b. Administer activated charcoal based on the child's weight. Diluting the poison now will help the child vomit thus eliminating much of the poison.
c. Administer O2 via nasal cannula and check the child's pupils for reactivity. The bump on the head may be the real issue.
d. Encourage the parents to immediately transport the child to their pediatrician for evaluation. A pediatrician is better trained to deal with pediatric emergencies.

Question 7: Your patient is a 33 year old female who fell off the back of a motorcycle going approximately 20 MPH. Her respirations are irregular at 8 a minute. An OPA has been inserted and ventilations are being assisted with a BVM and 100% O2 at a rate and tidal volume of_____. C-Spine precautions have been taken and she is packaged and moved to the ambulance where she stops breathing and there is no palpable pulse. CPR is started and the lead paramedic does a rapid sequence intubation. The BVM is attached to the ET tube and ventilations are restarted at a rate of _____.

a. 10 to 12 breaths per minute. Tidal volume of just enough air to give adequate chest rise. / 8 to 10 breaths per minute without pauses in compressions.
b. 10-12 breaths per minute. Tidal volume of approximately 800 ml. / 5-6 breaths per minute with pauses for ventilation delivery over 1 second.
c. 12 to 20 breaths per minute. Tidal volume of just enough air to make the chest rise with each ventilation. / 10-12 breaths per minute with no interruption of compressions to deliver ventilations.
d. 5 to 6 breaths per minute. Tidal volume of approximately 600 ml. / 8-10 breaths per minute with pauses to deliver compressions.

Question 8: Your patient is a 58 year old female. She called 911 complaining of difficulty breathing. During your initial assessment, you find that she is using accessory muscles to breath at a rate of 20 shallow breaths per minute, and her SpO2 is 98% on room air. She has high pitched inspiratory stridor and is slightly cyanotic around her mouth. When you kneel down beside her you notice an ash tray piled high with cigarette butts. Which of the following is the most likely cause of her breathing difficulty, and what would be the most appropriate treatment?

a. She likely has COPD and the swelling of her lower airway passages are causing the stridor. High flow O2 or nebulizer with rapid transport.
b. She has CHF and the fluid backing up into her lungs is causing the obstruction of her lower airway. The smoking likely worsened the condition. High flow 02 via NRB and transport
c. She has an upper airway obstruction. Do abdominal thrusts until the obstruction is free and then apply high flow O2 and transport
d. She has a foreign body obstruction in her upper airway. You should encourage her to cough in an attempt to dislodge it. Give high flow O2 and rapid transport

Question 9: Which of the following would not be considered an early sign of respiratory depression in a 7 year old girl?

a. Bobbing of the head
b. Retraction of the intercostals
c. Rapid respirations
d. Cyanosis of the lips

Question 10: What is Post Traumatic Stress Disorder (PTSD)?

a. Stress encountered after an incident
b. Effects on a broken leg during a transport down a rough road
c. The stress of being in combat
d. Stress encountered during an incident

Question 11: Which of the following choices is not a route of drug administration?

a. Nuchal
b. Inhaled
c. Intravenous
d. Sublingual

Question 12: You and your partner Stacy are called to an apartment complex for a 17 year old female complaining of abdominal pain. Upon entering the residence you see the patient looking pale and lying on the couch. Her abdomen is completely distended and she has a towel in her lap with traces of blood on it. Her respirations are at 20 breaths per minute and her pulse is 114. She denies any trauma and tells you she has a small amount of vaginal bleeding. After applying high flow O2 and moving her to the ambulance, you discover a loop of tissue protruding from the patients vagina. What is likely happening with this patient and how would you treat her?

a. She has preeclampsia with placenta abruptio. She should be transported in a left lateral recumbent position and treated for shock. Initiate IV therapy if scope of practice allows.
b. She is giving birth and has a nucal cord. Transport with the patient's head and torso down while monitoring vitals in route. Initiate IV therapy if scope of practice allows. If ETA is more than 30 minutes gently maneuver the cord back into the vagina.
c. She has an acute lower GI bleed and should be transported in a position of comfort and treated for shock. Establish IV if scope of practice allows.
d. She has a prolapsed cord. Insert a gloved hand into the vagina and check for pulsations in the cord. Gently lift child's head off of the cord and transport in a supine position with the hips elevated. Treat for shock and establish IV en route if scope of practice allows.

Question 13: You arrive on scene with your partner Elija to a multiple vehicle accident where you are the 2nd ambulance to arrive. Scene size up indicates there are 7 patients in 3 cars all requiring extrication. In the first car is a 27 year old woman who is 32 weeks pregnant, conscious, and crying, a 12 year old girl who is screaming and complaining of back pain, and an 8 year old boy who has a facial laceration and open fracture of the tibia who is also conscious but breathing very shallow. In the second car is an 86 year old man who is slumped against the steering wheel with no pulse and has a piece of metal impaled through his head. In the third car are 3 teenagers 17 years of age. The two in the front seat are complaining of neck pain and appear to have an altered level of consciousness. Neither of them were wearing a seatbelt and both have contusions on their foreheads. In the back seat is the last occupant, a girl who said she was having a seizure and vomiting earlier so her friends were taking her to the hospital. She was wearing her seat belt and has no sign of injury. Who should be receiving treatment first?

a. The pregnant woman
b. The 8 year old boy
c. The 86 year old man
d. The vomiting teenager

Question 14: A call comes in for a 61 yr old female with an altered LOC. When you arrive, the patient's sister tells you that the patient had a stroke about a year ago, but she knows of no other health problems. During your initial assessment, you find her eyes open and looking around. She is speaking to you, but saying inappropriate words. She will not obey your commands to "raise your arm please ma'am" and she moves her arm toward her chest when you give her a light sternal rub. What is this woman's GCS and what should you do after administering oxygen?

a. GCS of 12 / Package the patient for transport
b. GCS 7 / Get a BP, Pulse, and Respirations
c. GCS of 9 / Ask if she is taking any medications
d. GCS of 8 / Do a rapid assessment

Question 15: Fluid that accumulates in the lungs makes the transfer of oxygen more difficult as the alveoli are partitioned by the fluid. This condition is called?

a. Respiratory emesis
b. Alveoli failure
c. Pulmonary edema
d. Paradoxical flux

Question 16: Dispatch has just called you to Frontier Lake where a man's boat has capsized. The update is the patient is likely suffering from hypothermia and is breathing very shallow. You and your partner Sean arrive to find a man and a woman doing CPR on an approximately 48 year old male. When you and Sean begin CPR, what rate and depth of compressions will you use?

a. 30:2 / at least 2 inches
b. 15:2 / 1.5 to 2 inches
c. 30:15 / one third to one half the depth of the chest
d. 15:2 / one third to one half the depth of the chest

Question 17: You are the triage officer at a multiple casualty incident, and you are applying tags to each of the 5 patients. Patient 1 has a fractured tibia and is complaining of back pain. Patient 2 has a GCS of 6 with snoring respirations. Patient 3 has a broken finger. Patient 4 has no pulse and no respirations. Patient 5 has severe burns and a broken left radius. Which of the following choices provides the correct tag to patient combination?

a. 1Red, 2Yellow, 3Red, 4Yellow, 5Black
b. 1Yellow, 2Red, 3Green, 4Black, 5Red
c. 1Yellow, 2Yellow, 3Green, 4Red, 5Red
d. 1Red, 2Yellow, 3Black, 4Green, 5Red

Question 18: Your patient has a distended abdomen which you know can disrupt proper movement of the diaphragm and lead to?

a. Hyperventilation
b. Hyperglycemia
c. Pleurisy
d. Hypoventilation

Question 19: How many compressions per minute would you give an adult patient who has no pulse?

a. 80-100 compressions per minute
b. 100-120 compressions per minute
c. 60-80 compressions per minute
d. 30-2 compressions per minute

Question 20: You and your partner Zoe arrive on scene to find an 8 year old girl who was struck by an ice cream truck while crossing the street. She is unresponsive and has an abrasion on her forehead and an abrasion on her right side. She is breathing at 20 breaths per minute with adequate depth. What would be the most appropriate action to take at this point?

a. Take C-spine precautions and Administer O2 via nasal canula at 6 LPM
b. Do a rapid trauma assessment and call law enforcement
c. Start positive pressure ventilations with a BVM at 12-20 breaths per minute
d. Give her a sternal rub to check for responsiveness and bandage the abrasions

Question 21: An Incident Command System is designed to:

a. Notify emergency personnel about the level of triage to expect
b. Stabilize patients of a mass casualty
c. Define the roles and responsibilities of an EMS system
d. Manage and control emergency responders and resources

Question 22: You are about to begin CPR on a patient .You go to open their airway when you realize that CPR will probably not be advised. Which of the following answers could be a reason not to administer CPR?

a. The patient is unconscious and not breathing
b. The patient has hot, dry skin
c. The patient has no pulse or respirations
d. The patient has a stiff neck and jaw

Question 23: Your patient doesn't remember what happened. She is sweating, incontinent, and has a bleeding tongue. What do you suspect happened to this patient?

a. The patient overdosed on medications
b. The patient was struck in the head by a baseball
c. The patient is hypoglycemic
d. The patient experienced a seizure

Question 24: You and your partner Aaron arrive on scene to find a 10 year old boy who was struck by a car while chasing a cat into the street. He is unresponsive to painful stimuli and has a large abrasion on his right side. He is breathing at 24 respirations per minute and regular. Your next course of action would be...?

a. Give high flow O2 with an NRB
b. Initiate CPR
c. Start bagging him with a BVM
d. Put a C collar on him

Question 25: You are the lone EMT stationed at a local sporting event when you witness a man collapse from an apparent cardiac arrest. You have all of the equipment that you would need for a cardiac arrest event with you. Your best course of action would be?

a. Immediately do CPR for 2 minutes and then retrieve the AED
b. Attach the AED, hook it up, and analyze
c. Call ALS, do 5 cycles of CPR, retrieve the AED
d. Check for a pulse and breathing, retrieve the AED

Question 26: What is the first stage of labor?

a. The baby crowns
b. The baby is in the birth canal
c. The cervix is dilating
d. The placenta is delivered

Question 27: Approximately how many ambulance crashes happen each year in the United States?

a. 1,000
b. 3,000
c. 6,000
d. 12,000

Question 28: You are transporting a 27-year-old female who was the driver in a single car MVA on a remote logging road. She is on oxygen at 12LPM and had an actively bleeding laceration on her scalp that has been controlled with pressure. Her pulse is 100 with respirations of 12 a minute and her blood pressure is 110/70. You are still 30 to 40 minutes from the hospital. According to the NREMT trauma management skill sheet, which of the following answer choices contains the best treatment for this patient given the circumstances.

a. Put a C-collar on her and re-assess vitals every 15 minutes en route
b. Perform a secondary assessment of the laceration to make sure bleeding has stopped
c. Assess airway, breathing, and circulation every 5 minutes until arrival at the hospital
d. Reassess and treat any conditions that present

Question 29: You arrive on scene with your partner Steve to a 1-vehicle accident. You are the 1st ambulance to arrive. Scene size up indicates there are 4 patients in the car. In the front is a 45 year old woman who is unconscious and wearing her seat belt, a 7 year old girl who is unrestrained and complaining of finger pain, an 8 year old boy who is unrestrained and has no signs or symptoms, and a 5 year old girl who is unrestrained and has no signs or symptoms. There is little to no damage to the car and it appears as if she just went off the road at a very slow rate of speed and bumped up against a fence. What could have likely been the cause of the woman's altered LOC?

a. Diabetic reaction, alcohol, stroke, or seizure
b. Poisoning, exhaust in the car, or head trauma
c. Coma, AMI, or GI bleed
d. Carbon monoxide poisoning, anaphylaxis, or pneumothorax

Question 30: Your 57 year old patient was a chain smoker for 35 years and is pursing his lips during exhalation. How does this action assist the patients respiratory effort?

a. It creates a backpressure on collapsed alveoli
b. It forces air out of the lungs faster
c. It demonstrates their lung control
d. It causes them to hyperventilate

Question 31: An ice storm has caused a 10 car pile up on a nearby interstate. Incident command has instructed you to take over triage of the patients. Patient 1 is a woman who has a broken arm and a back injury with suspected spinal cord damage. Patient 2 is male and has a broken femur and is showing signs of shock. Patient 3 is an elderly woman who has a laceration on her forehead and pain in her wrist. Patient 4 is a male, breathing at 6 breaths a minute with a head injury. What color triage tag should each of these patients receive?

a. 1Red, 2Red, 3Black, 4Red
b. 1Yellow, 2Yellow, 3Green, 4Black
c. 1Green, 2Red, 3Black, 4Red
d. 1Yellow, 2Red, 3Green, 4Red

Question 32: You and your partner are at lunch when you are called to a scene of a 3 yr old who does not have a pulse and is not breathing. You and your partner discuss what depth of compression should be given and you agree that it is?

a. 1-2 inches
b. 1.5-2.5 inches
c. At least 1/3rd the depth of the chest
d. No compressions, it's a child

Question 33: The body's first physiological response to a deep laceration is _____.

a. To stop it by chemical means and vasoconstriction (hemostasis)
b. To stop it by means of slowing the heart and respirations
c. Psychogenic shock
d. Decorticate posturing

Question 34: Dispatch reports a jet ski collision on a local lake. The reporting party says that the two guys are in the water floating face down and one of their buddies just jumped off the boat to help them. When you arrive on scene the boat has just brought the two unconscious men to shore and CPR and rescue breathing are in progress. The first man has a pulse but is not breathing. The second man does not have a pulse and is apneic. What ventilation rate will you use for the first man? What about the second man?

a. 30:2 compression to ventilation ratio for both men
b. 30 compressions to 2 ventilations per minute for both men
c. 12-20 ventilations per minute for the first man and 10-12 ventilations per minute for the second man
d. 10-12 ventilations per minute for the first man and 6 ventilations per minute and 100 compressions for the second man

Question 35: You respond to a call of a house fire where the first unit on scene has reported burn injuries to a child that are classified as "minor". Minor burns for a child would be?

a. Partial thickness burns over the anterior trunk
b. Full thickness burns on less than 2% of the body
c. Partial thickness burn on one hand and one foot
d. Partial thickness burns on one arm

Question 36: You arrive on scene of a shooting where law enforcement has secured the scene. Which of the following answers contain the most accurate sequence of actions according to the NREMT trauma management skill sheet?

a. Determine the number of patients - Consider C-spine stabilization - Assess the patient's airway - Get a set of vital signs
b. BSI - Determine the MOI - Get a sample history - Do a secondary assessment on the wound - Make transport decision
c. General impression of the patient - Make transport decision - Treat life threats - Get a set of vital signs
d. BSI - Direct pressure on the wound - Assess airway - Transport decision - Get vital signs

Question 37: What life-threatening disease is caused by abnormally low levels of corticosteroid hormones produced by the adrenal glands which causes weight loss, weakness, hypotension, and gastrointestinal disorders?

a. Cushing Syndrome
b. Addison Disease
c. Thyrotoxicosis
d. Thyroid Storm

Question 38: You are responding the the scene of a possible drowning. Dispatch resports that a 3 year old girl was found face down in the family swimming pool. In this case the use of lights and sirens would be:

a. Used for clearing traffic in front of you so you can get to the scene more rapidly
b. Standing operating procedures for pediatric patients
c. To warn other drivers that you are moving rapidly toward an emergency and to use caution.
d. Used as a device to ask other drivers for the right-of-way

Question 39: A 6 year old child has fallen from the monkey bars at the local park. What are the components of the pediatric assessment triangle (PAT) that you would use to rapidly assess this patient?

a. Airway, Breathing, and Circulation
b. Appearance, Work of breathing, Circulation
c. Mentation, Reaction, Distress level
d. General impression, Distress level, Transport priority level

Question 40: A respiration rate would be considered within normal limits for an adult at_____ per minute, for a 6-12 year old child at _____ per minute, and for an infant at_____ per minute.

a. 22 - 32 - 42
b. 16 - 25 - 40
c. 20 - 40 - 60
d. 10 - 20 - 40

Question 41: You have just assisted in the delivery of a baby boy. The child is pink, but his arms and legs are blue. His pulse rate is 90 beats per minute. He is not making any sound and is showing limited movement. His respirations are slow and irregular. What is this newborn's APGAR score and how should he be treated?

a. 3 / Stimulate the baby with a gentle swat to the buttocks while holding him upside down. Wrap him in clean dry towels and place on the mother's stomach to keep warm.

b. 4 / Stimulate the newborn by rubbing his spine. Use clean towels to dry him off and place him at the level of the mother's vagina.

c. 5 / Begin ventilations via BVM with 100% oxygen until the baby

d. 6 / Continue suctioning the mouth and then the nose until the baby's arms and legs turn pink. Use blow by oxygen and wrap the baby in warm clean towels.

Question 42: Which type of diabetic emergency generally has a rapid onset?

a. Diabetic coma
b. DKA
c. Hypoglycemia
d. Viperglycemic

Question 43: You have requested helicopter transportation of a critical burn patient. The remote nature of the accident will force the helicopter to land on an incline. From which direction should you approach the helicopter?

a. The back
b. The front
c. The uphill side
d. The downhill side

Question 44: Someone who is U on the AVPU scale would require what type of secondary assessment?

a. Rapid full-body scan
b. Focused physical
c. UP assessment
d. QUICK assessment

Question 45: A fierce winter storm has left hundreds of people stranded along a stretch of highway for a few days. You have been dispatched with the National Guard to help care for anyone suffering from exposure. As you prepare your equipment what things should you carry extra of and why?

a. Blankets; Any patients you meet will need aggressive warming and blankets are part of that
b. Drinking water; Dehydration is a very likely problem
c. Warm IV fluids; The patients will need warm IV fluids to help combat the hypothermia you will likely encounter
d. Oral glucose; If patients have not had food for a few days they may have low blood glucose levels

Question 46: You are preparing to suction secretions from your patient's airway, when would you engage the suction action in the catheter?

a. When inserting the catheter and while suctioning secretions
b. While suctioning secretions and withdrawing the catheter
c. From the time the catheter tip passes the lips going in, until it passes the lips coming out
d. For no more than 10 seconds

Question 47: Unoxygenated blood travels into the lungs via the?

a. Pulmonary valve
b. Pulmonary artery
c. Pulmonary vein
d. Aortic arch

Question 48: Which of the following is NOT considered a common side effect of nitroglycerin?

a. Bradypnea
b. Increased heart rate
c. Weakness
d. Headache

Question 49: Who is responsible for developing protocols for an EMS system?

a. Department of Transportation (DOT)
b. Medical director
c. State EMS Control
d. National EMS control

Question 50: Name three medical conditions that often cause tachypnea?

a. Hypoxia, CHF, shock
b. Fibromyalgia, hypoxia, ischemia
c. Hypoxia, congestive heart failure, opiate overdose
d. Allergic reaction, shock, CHF

Question 51: You arrive at an apartment building where a man has been reported unconscious. You enter the room to find him lying supine in his bed with his wife at his side. Respirations are rapid and shallow at 24 breaths per minute and you are unable to get a response from him. His wife says he is a diabetic and that she just lanced his finger to measure his glucose when you arrived. What would be the best course of action?

a. Give him a tube of glucose - Administer high flow 02 via NRB, and transport
b. High flow 02 - Have the wife finish measuring the blood sugar - Transport
c. Start positive pressure ventilations at 10-12 per minute - attach high flow O2, and transport
d. Administer high flow O2 Assess circulation - Make a transport decision

Question 52: Dispatch has called you and your partner Libby to an ATV accident in the foothills of a nearby mountain range. You come on scene to find a 60 yr old man lying in a weeded area off to the side of the road. He apparently lost control of the four wheeler and it rolled several times. According to the NREMT spinal immobilization skill sheet, which of the following answer choices contain your MOST accurate sequence of steps?

a. BSI - Direct assistant to put head in inline position - Apply C-collar - Directs movement of patient onto board
b. Direct assistant to maintain manual immobilization of the head - Check circulation and motor sensory - Apply C -collar
c. BSI - Check circulation motor sensory - Direct assistant to put head in inline position - Directs movement to backboard
d. Direct assistant to maintain manual immobilization of the head - Direct assistant to place head in inline position - Check CMS - Transport decision

Question 53: You are called to the scene of a woman who is having difficulty breathing. Upon arrival you notice several people surrounding the woman who seems to be agitated. Your scene assessment determines it to be safe and you approach the woman who is in the tripod position. Her breathing is rapid and shallow. She states her ribs hurt after being struck with a punch from her husband. You should?

a. Call law enforcement and leave the scene until they arrive
b. Treat the patient if the situation appears safe and inform law enforcement of the possible assault when the time is appropriate
c. Call the husband out for hitting a woman and make him look dumb in front of the rest of the family
d. Inform the woman that she will have to go to the hospital if she wants to get treated. This environment is not safe

Question 54: You are assessing the vital signs of a 7-year-old child. Which of the following sets of vitals would you hope to find?

a. BP 104/60, respirations of 16 per minute and a pulse of 98
b. BP 116/70, respirations of 27 per minute and a pulse of 130
c. BP 108/64, respirations of 20 per minute and a pulse of 100
d. BP 100/58, respirations of 14 per minute and a pulse of 125

Question 55: You and your partner Warren arrive at a house where a woman in her 50's has been reported unconscious. Her pulse is 80 and she is apneic. Warren inserts an oropharyngeal and you begin ventilating her at _____. After about 1 minute of ventilations, the patient begins to have seizures and is gagging. What would be the most appropriate thing to do?

a. 10-12 breaths per minute / insert a nasopharyngeal
b. 12-20 breaths per minute / Prepare to suction
c. 10-12 breaths per minute/ Remove the oropharyngeal
d. 12-20 breaths per minute / Begin suctioning her airway

Question 56: You arrive on scene to find a female patient actively having contractions every 10-12 minutes apart. A visual inspection of the patient reveals no visible crowning. Which stage of labor would you consider this patient to be in?

a. 1st stage of labor.
b. 2nd stage of labor.
c. 3rd stage of labor
d. 4th stage of labor

Question 57: You are dispatched on a medical call to a 45 year old male who is exhibiting signs of a stroke. His wife told dispatch that her husband's speech is slurred and he appears to be having seizures. When you arrive on scene, the man is sweating profusely in a postictal state and breathing at 16 breaths a minute with adequate volume and regularity. What elements of the assessment would likely be the most useful right now?

a. Glascow coma scale and pulse rate
b. History and blood glucose measurement
c. Patent airway established and blood pressure
d. Baseline vitals and a rapid physical exam

Question 58: You are called to a neighborhood pool where a 5 year old girl was found floating unconscious. She is cyanotic and has no muscle tone. Your partner Greg does not find a pulse and the child is not breathing. Your CPR should include a compression to ventilation ratio of_____ and each compression should be at a depth of_____.

a. 30:2 / one third the diameter of the chest
b. 15:2 / one third the diameter of the chest
c. 30:2 / 1.5 to 2 inches in depth
d. 15:2 / just enough to give adequate chest rise

Question 59: You have been called to a bowling alley for an unknown medical. A 50ish male is lying supine in the parking lot and there is a crowd of people around him. There is no sign of trauma. He is breathing deep, regular, and rapid with his arms crossed over his chest. There is a small puddle of orange colored vomit next to his head. He will not respond to you and his pants are saturated with what appears to be urine. There is a full bottle of whiskey laying next to him on the cement. What is most likely wrong with this man, and what would be the best choice of treatment?

a. He is likely hypoglycemic as alcohol lowers blood sugar levels. A tube of glucose and a blood sugar check should be administered
b. He was hit by a car driving through the parking lot. C-collar, backboard, and rapid transport.
c. He is a diabetic who ran out of insulin and now he is hyperglycemic. A fluid bolis and oxygen via NRB
d. He has had a syncopal episode as the result of a drug overdose. Insert an OPA and provide positive pressure ventilation

Question 60: Which of the following would you expect to find in an infant who is breathing adequately?

a. Use of accessory muscles
b. Belly breathing
c. Respirations of 15 a minute
d. Retraction of the intercostal muscles

Question 61: NIMS is best explained as:

a. A National system of managing large emergencies based on having private and governmental organizations work independently at the scene of a mass casualty
b. A systematic approach of assessment used during the triage of large groups of people during a mass casualty incident
c. Governmental rescue organizations taking responsibility for controlling the parts of the scene that fall within their expertise
d. A template system for providing consistent, effective processes in preparing for, responding to, and recovering from an incident

Question 62: You and your partner Asher arrive on scene to find a woman who has had a syncopal episode at her daughter's wedding. It was brought on, she says, by witnessing for the first time a dragon tattoo on the ankle of her daughter as she walked down the isle. Guests at the wedding state that she was eased to the ground and did not fall and hit anything. After laying supine for 10 minutes she was helped to her feet with no complaints. She is pale, but has all function and has a GCS of 15. This woman likely suffered what?

a. Psychogenic shock
b. Cardiogenic shock
c. Neurogenic shock
d. Hemotastic shock

Question 63: It's 20 degrees outside and your unit has been called to an apartment complex where a man is having trouble breathing. You arrive to find the man sitting in a tripod position on a bench. He has a portable O2 tank and is receiving oxygen via a nasal cannula at 3 LPM. Your initial assessment reveals that his breathing is rapid with minimal chest rise and fall. Respiration rate is 20 breaths per minute and his pulse is 130. In a hoarse voice the man tells you he has a history of COPD and is on a new medication which he is unable to name. He denies any chest pain, but says he is getting a headache. Which of the following scenarios is most likely the cause for this man's breathing difficulties and how would you treat him?

a. He is having an allergic reaction to the new COPD medication. Move him to the ambulance and administer high flow 02 via NRB

b. His COPD medication is not the correct dosage and it is not clearing the surfactant from the alveolar walls. Move him to the ambulance and put him on high flow O2 via his cannula.

c. He is going into anaphylaxis as a result of a bee sting. Inject him with an Epi pen and check his vitals in the back of the ambulance.

d. He has pneumonia from his COPD and being out in the cold. Actively warm him in the back of the ambulance and transport him to the nearest hospital

Question 64: Why does the NHTSA require use of lights and sirens during response and transportation?

a. The safety of EMS providers and public is the driving force of the NHTSA

b. The NHTSA does NOT require use of lights and sirens during response and transportation

c. NHTSA research has shown that every second counts in the outcome of patients

d. High visibility decreases the likelihood of a vehicle accident

Question 65: You and your partner Genovese suspect a significant MOI to a patient who has been in a high-speed front end collision. In what order should you do your assessment?

a. Primary survey - SAMPLE history - Secondary assessment

b. SAMPLE history - Rapid trauma assessment - Focused physical

c. Vital signs - SAMPLE history - Secondary survey

d. Focused trauma - SAMPLE - Baseline vitals

Question 66: You respond to a call of a man down in a very rough neighborhood. Upon entering the location of the call you notice a group of young men in a fist fight at what appears to be the address of the call. There are two men on the ground not moving and your lights and sirens have frightened the other men away. What should you do next?

a. Call for police to secure the scene and wait for them to arrive

b. Treat the patient with the worst injuries first

c. Check to see if they have a weapon

d. Chase down the slowest guy and hold him for the police

Question 67: You arrive on scene with your partner Zelda to a restaurant where a woman is apparently having a reaction to the seafood from the buffet. She is having trouble breathing and her lips are swollen. Zelda hands you an adult EPI pen and you inject the patient into the thigh and hold it there for about 10 seconds. How long will the injection likely be effective?

a. 30-60 minutes

b. 1-2 hours

c. 10-20 minutes

d. 24 hours

Question 68: Your local Emergency Medical System is regulated by:

a. The National Registry of Emergency Medical Technicians.
b. Your medical director.
c. The National Highway Traffic Safety Administration.
d. Your state EMS office.

Question 69: A woman has fallen 20 ft. from a ski lift. You are the first medical unit on scene. She is conscious and breathing normally. C spine is in place and you package her on a backboard with high flow O2 and begin transport. The patient is looking around the ambulance and begins using inappropriate words to describe things she is seeing. You have given her several requests to wiggle her toes but she does not respond. This woman has a GCS of what?

a. 8
b. 9
c. 10
d. 11

Question 70: Without any further information, what condition would you say the following patient is in? A 1-year-old male with a pulse rate of 110, breathing at 30 breaths per minute, with a systolic BP of 90.

a. Good
b. Poor
c. Bad
d. Moderate

Question 71: Your patient was the restrained passenger in a vehicle accident. She is complaining of back pain and shortness of breath. The proper way to remove this patient from the car is?

a. Using a seated immobilization device and then moving her to a backboard
b. Rapid extrication while maintaining c-spine precautions
c. With 2 EMTs in the car and 2 outside the car
d. Splinting any fractures and transitioning her out on a backboard

Question 72: You are dispatched to a boat fire with multiple victims in the water. You are the only Paramedic on scene. Upon arrival you find patient #1 shivering uncontrollably, but able to answer questions appropriately. Patient #2 is on a boat across the bay with another EMS unit. That unit relates that the patient is mildly hypothermic and doesn't want to be transported. Both patients indicate that a third person was with them and that he was burned badly. On scene command confirms that this patient is still in the water. Which is the most critical patient, and why?

a. Patient #1, because she is in severe hypothermia.
b. Patient #2, because he can't reason properly.
c. Patient #3, because he will require the most care when he is removed from the water.
d. Patient #1, because she is in hypogenic shock.

Question 73: You arrive on scene and find an elderly man who has a history of hypertension. He takes medication daily for it to be regulated. He is feeling dizzy, his pulse is 70 and his BP is 110/70. Which is the most likely cause of his symptoms?

a. He is in shock
b. He has had a heart attack
c. He has likely not taken his medication
d. He is hypertensive

Question 74: You and your partner Domonica are called to the scene of a single car MVA with two patients. The reporting party told dispatch that one of the patients is unconscious in the car and the other is out of the car and conscious, but bleeding badly from his face. You arrive to find that the man in the car is actually dead and the other man is standing up against a bystander's car. According to the NREMT Patient Assessment/Management - Trauma Skill Sheet what would be the most appropriate treatment for this patient?

a. Verbalize general impression of the patient, Determine chief complaint/apparent life threats, Make a transport decision, and get a set of baseline vitals
b. Determine chief complaint, do a secondary assessment, Treat ABC's, and then make a transport decision based on the vitals
c. BSI, Treat any life threats, Do a detailed focused exam, Check vital signs and make a transport decision
d. Consider stabilization of the spine, Perform a primary survey and make a transport decision, then do a secondary assessment

Question 75: You are dispatched to a daycare where a child is having difficulty breathing. The caregiver called 911 and reported that the 5-year-old went down for a nap. When she went to check on him 30 minutes later he did not appear to be breathing normally. En route to this call, what are the most important things to remember?

a. Sunken fontanelles can indicate dehydration or possible allergic reaction. Wheezing respirations with red skin may also indicate swelling in the throat.
b. Daycare providers are often involved with child abuse. Remember to look for odd shaped bruising or burns on the child. Note if the caregiver is acting oddly or has difficulty making eye contact with you.
c. Because of the size of a child's head you may need additional padding under the shoulders to align the airway. Flexion and hyperextension can obstruct the airway.
d. Caregivers may be reluctant to give additional information about the cause of the child's respiratory difficulty out of fear of blame. Call law enforcement if you suspect abuse.

Question 76: Your unit is called to the scene of a motor vehicle collision at a busy intersection. A man in his 40's, driving a small truck, has hit a telephone pole head on. He was unrestrained and ejected through the windshield at approximately 50 MPH. When you arrive, he has been secured to a backboard with proper c-spine precautions. His pulse is 80 beats per minute and he is breathing regularly and deeply at 12 respirations per minute. You notice that his pulse seems to weaken during inhalation. While taking his blood pressure, you see that each time he inhales, his systolic pressure drops by 20-30 mmHg. His trachea is midline and lung sounds are equal. What is the most likely reason for these vital signs?

a. Head injuries involving the pons portion of the brain often cause patients to exhibit irregular breathing patterns and irregular pulses.
b. Liquid filling the pericardium increases pressure and inhibits the ventricles from filling properly, which in turn leads to low stroke volume and low pressure
c. Air has begun filling the pleural space through a hole in the chest inhibiting the lungs from filling with air. This in turn puts pressure on the heart, causing the pressure to fluctuate with each inspiration
d. Injury to the spine may interfere with signals sent from the medulla oblongata to the diaphragm. This interference

causes a variant or irregular breathing pattern and consequent drop in blood pressure

Question 77: You and your partner Ramone have arrived at the scene of a house fire where 3 victims were pulled a safe distance from the home and are being attended by first responders. Your initial impression is of two women and a child lying unconscious on the ground. None appears to have been burned and their clothing is intact. None of the patients is breathing, but the second woman and the child do have a palpable pulse. At what rate would each of these patients be ventilated?

a. Woman one would get 6 breaths per minute. Woman two would get 12 to 20 breaths per minute and the child would get 15 to 30 breaths per minute

b. Woman one would get 12 breaths over 2 minutes. Woman two would get 20 to 24 breaths over 2 minutes and the child would get 24 to 40 breaths over 2 minutes

c. Woman one would get 10 to 12 breaths per minute. Woman two would get 12 to 20 breaths per minute and the child would get 12 to 20 breaths per minute

d. Woman one would get 12 to 20 breaths per minute. Woman two would get 12 to 20 breaths per minute and the child would get 15 to 30 breaths per minute

Question 78: A woman's obstetrical history can be displayed using P and G. How would you display a woman's history who has had 3 pregnancies and 2 live births?

a. P-3 - G-2

b. P3G-2

c. G3P3

d. G3P2

Question 79: A 46-year-old woman was hiking in the woods near her home when she accidentally stepped into a hive of hornets and was stung multiple times. She contacted 911 via her cell phone and is going to rendezvous with you at her residence. When you arrive at the home you find her lying on the front lawn. After completing your scene size up, which would be the most appropriate treatment sequence according to the NREMT Patient Assessment/Management - Medical Skill Sheet?

a. Form a general impression - Assist with epinephrine via auto injector - High flow O2 - and transport

b. Administer high flow O2 via NRB - Get a set of vitals - and then do a SAMPLE

c. Determine level of consciousness - Identify life threats - Assess airway - breathing - and circulation

d. Assess ABC's - Make a transport decision and do a secondary assessment on the respiratory system. If she appears to be in anaphylactic shock assist her with her epinephrine auto injector.

Question 80: You and your partner Abraham arrive on scene to a one-car collision with a cow. Your patient was driving about 45 MPH around a corner when the cow leaped from the roadside in front of the car. After doing your initial scene size up, which of the following would you proceed to?

a. Baseline vitals

b. Get a general impression of the patient

c. Perform a detailed physical examination

d. C spine and SAMPLE history with focused physical examination

Question 81: What would be an expected systolic BP in infants, toddlers, and preschool aged children?

a. 50 mm Hg
b. 60 mm Hg
c. 70 mm Hg
d. 80 mm Hg

Question 82: A 27 year old man and his 4 year old nephew have been pulled from a river after being submerged for approximately 12 minutes. Rescue breathing for the man should include breaths at what rate? Rescue breathing for the child should include breaths at what rate?

a. 1 breath every 5-6 seconds for the man / 1 breath every 3-5 seconds for the child
b. 12-20 breaths per minute for the man / 10-12 breaths per minute for the child
c. 10-12 breaths per minute for the man / 20-30 breaths per minute for all children
d. 1 breath every 3-5 seconds for the man / 1 breath every 5-6 seconds for the child

Question 83: You and your partner Grimes are called to the scene of a stabbing. There are two patients reported. A woman with a stab wound to the URQ and a man with a stab wound to the LRQ. The woman with the wound in the URQ is having problems breathing, has a pulse of 103, respirations of 35, and they are shallow. The patient with the stab wound to the LRQ is complaining of severe abdominal pain and has a pulse of 48 and a respiration rate of 24. Which patient is most likely to have a low blood pressure? Why?

a. The man, because of the nature and location of the injury, he may be losing blood internally. His pulse is too slow as well
b. The woman, because if she cannot breathe well her BP will drop
c. The man, because a respiration rate of 24 is indicative of low blood pressure
d. Neither will have a low blood pressure, they will both be high

Question 84: What would a baby that had a cephalic presentation during birth be considered?

a. An emergency
b. A reason for a c section
c. Unlikely to be healthy
d. Optimal for delivery

Question 85: A call has come in for a possible drowning. You and your partner respond to a public swimming pool a few blocks from the station. A 9 year old boy apparently slipped while running, hit his head on the edge of the pool, and fell in. He has no pulse and he is not breathing. What would be your best choice of action?

a. Apply a cervical collar and begin respirations and compressions at a 30:2 ratio. Deliver breaths with a BVM at 12-20 breaths per minute.
b. Insert an oropharyngeal measured from the corner of his mouth to his earlobe and begin assisting ventilations at 15-30 breaths per minute.
c. Take mechanical c-spine precautions and begin CPR delivering 5-6 breaths per minute while giving 100 compressions in that same time period.
d. Take manual stabilization of the boy's head and neck while additional rescuers ventilate at about 13 breaths per minute and provide at least 100 compressions per minute.

Question 86: Which of the following statements is correct regarding the operation of an emergency vehicle:

a. Emergency vehicles have certain limited privileges in every state which protects them from liability in a crash
b. Emergency vehicles should only pass school buses when they have stopped to load children
c. Pedestrians and drivers in all states are required to give emergency vehicles the right of way
d. Emergency vehicles must always be operated with due regard for the safety of others

Question 87: What are the main differences between a child's airway and an adult's airway?

a. A child's airway is shorter and more compact than an adult's, making it easier to visualize the vocal cords
b. An adult's airway is more narrow than a child's airway
c. A child's airway is narrower at the Cricoid ring and the tongue is larger in proportion to the mouth
d. There is no difference. Children's airways are just like adults

Question 88: You and your partner Larry are dispatched to the call of a man with sever stomach pain. When you arrive on scene you find him lying on the floor of the kitchen in the fetal position. There is vomit on his face and he says he is going to throw up again. He denies falling and says the only thing wrong is that his stomach is killing him. Assessing his abdomen you find it to be very tender to the touch and he moans when you palpate his stomach. He is also breathing very fast at 30 a minute. What other signs and symptoms might you find with this patient?

a. Tachycardia - hypotension - fever
b. Bottle of poison, cyanosis, and crepitus
c. Broken ribs, hypertension, and deep, rapid breathing
d. Rebound tenderness - metabolic acidosis

Question 89: You arrive on scene to find a man in his 20's lying in a pool of vomit. You can see that he is breathing at about 16 breaths per minute and the depth of respiration is adequate. He has a small laceration on his forehead. You try getting a response by calling "Hey man can you hear me?" but he does not answer. Your partner gives him a quick sternal rub and his eyes pop open along with a whimper under his breath and then they close again. You ask him to perform several motor functions but he does not comply. He does not answer any of your questions. This man has a GCS of what?

a. 14
b. 9
c. 4
d. 7

Question 90: The symptoms of a TIA usually last around _____.

a. 1 minute
b. An hour
c. 24 hours
d. 48 hours

Question 91: You and your partner are called to a swimming pool for a 5 year old who does not have a pulse and is not breathing. You begin CPR including compressions at what depth?

a. 2 inches
b. 1.5-3 inches
c. At least 1/3 the diameter of the chest
d. 1/2 to one third the depth of the chest

Question 92: You have just arrived at the scene to find a 27-year-old female complaining of anxiety and breathing difficulties. Which of the following questions would be most appropriate to ask first?

a. What is your name?
b. What day is today?
c. Do you have a history of panic attacks?
d. How long have you been having trouble breathing?

Question 93: EMT B Maloney is moving from an ambulance service in one state to a new ambulance service in another state. His new unit will accept his state license as an EMT B. This is an example of?

a. Multiple licensure
b. Reciprocity
c. National Certification
d. Probationary acceptance

Question 94: You arrive on scene with your partner Joe to find an 7 year old boy unconscious after being dragged from the water. He is not breathing and has no pulse. CPR in this case should include_____.

a. 30:2 compression to ventilation ratio
b. 15:2 compression to ventilation ratio
c. 5:1 compression to ventilation ratio
d. 30:1 compression to ventilation ratio

Question 95: In order to manuever an ambulance efficiently around a turn the driver should know the proper speed, _____ as well as understand the need to

_____.

a. the desired ending point of the turn / reach the apex of the turn early
b. the current position and projected path / reach the apex late in the turn
c. the caliper and approximate distance of the turn / begin turning early in the turn
d. how tight the turn is / apply the breaks if the turn was entered with too much speed

Question 96: You are transporting a 6 year old child that has had a seizure. She is in the postictal state. How would you best describe this patient?

a. The patient is sleeping comfortably and is easy to rouse
b. The patient has weakness on one side of the body and acts as if they have had a stroke
c. The patient is unresponsive with deep and rapid respirations
d. The patient is combative and wants to fight you

Question 97: You arrive at a restaurant to a call of a woman choking. You find her sitting in a chair, very pale, and sweating. She states in a very hush tone that she has a piece of steak caught in her throat. You should immediately?

a. Give her the Heimlich and pop the chunk of steak out
b. Tell her she should not take such big bites
c. Wait until she passes out and then give her abdominal compressions on the ground
d. Encourage her to cough as it is likely high enough in the airway to expel it

Question 98: You have been unsuccessful in starting an IV on a 2 year old child that is in cardiac arrest. Your medical direction indicates you should consider initiating IO access to administer medications. As you prepare this procedure what are the anatomical landmarks you are looking for, and what are the complication risks with this procedure?

a. distal tibia / fracture of the tibia
b. proximal tibia / pulmonary embolism
c. distal fibula / compartment syndrome
d. proximal fibula / severe pain

Question 99: Which set contains parts of the lower airway only?

a. Pharynx, larynx, lungs, and diaphragm
b. Mouth, epiglottis, trachea, and bronchi
c. Nose, alveoli, bronchi, and diaphragm
d. Trachea, alveoli, bronchi, and bronchioles

Question 100: A DNR is?

a. A dual lumen airway device
b. Not legal to use in all states
c. An advanced directive
d. Only valid if notarized

Question 101: The umbilical cord is wrapped tightly around the baby's neck and you have tried unsuccessfully to slip the cord over the head. What should your next course of action be?

a. Push the baby's head into the vagina until the cord comes loose
b. Clamp the cord in two places and cut it in the middle
c. Support the head and suction the baby's nose and mouth
d. Massage the uterus to stimulate harder contractions to free the baby

Question 102: You arrive on scene to find a 78 year old man who is sitting in a chair and staring off into space. His breathing is labored and you can hear wet lung sounds. You get no answer when you try to get his name. Your requests for him to move his toes go without response. Immediate treatment for this patient would include _____.

a. Aggressive IV therapy
b. Transporting in a supine position
c. High flow O2
d. Administration of epinephrine

Question 103: If a Paramedic instructs you to hyperventilate the patient prior to intubation, what would you do?

a. Coach the patient to breath faster
b. Assist ventilations with 100% oxygen for several minutes
c. Nothing, because that would be dangerous and constitute negligence
d. Turn the O2 up to 25 lpm and adjust the mask

Question 104: After the baby's head has delivered you should?

a. Suction the mouth and nose then check if the cord is wrapped around the infant's neck
b. Suction the mouth and nose and wait for the mother to push the rest of the baby out
c. Support the head and gently pull the baby out
d. Put the mother on high flow O2 and prepare to deliver the rest of the infant.

Question 105: You arrive on scene to find a 57 year old man who is sitting on a couch appearing to stare at the wall. His breathing is labored and you can hear wet breath sounds that are producing a pink foam dripping from his mouth. You get no response when you try to get his name. Your requests for him to move his arm go without response. His pulse is 105 and his BP is 92/40. You do not see any edema, swelling, or JVD. This patient likely has _____.

a. Left sided CHF
b. Hypoglycemia
c. Right sided CHF
d. Appendicitis

Question 106: You are dispatched to a home for a laceration. A 60 yr old male was chopping wood with a hatchet when he missed and hit his wrist. When you make patient contact, his wrist is still actively bleeding. Which of the following treatment sequences would be the MOST appropriate ?

a. Elevate wounded extremity - Direct Pressure to wound - Apply tourniquet
b. BSI - Apply pressure to arterial pressure point - Elevate wounded extremity - Apply tourniquet
c. Direct pressure - tourniquet
d. BSI - High flow O2 - Arterial pressure on pressure point - transport

Question 107: A woman who is multigravida but primipara would have?

a. Had multiple pregnancies with two live births
b. Had multiple pregnancies with one live birth
c. Had multiple live births
d. Had multiple pregnancies and multiple births

Question 108: Meconium is:

a. A sign of a lower GI bleed. Dark colored stool as the result of digested blood.
b. Often found in amniotic fluid when the fetus has voided in the womb.
c. A natural lubricant produced in the uterus to aid in delivery of the fetus.
d. Is an alternative to Nitro and should only be used if local protocols allow.

Question 109: A 6 year old girl was found outside in her yard unconscious. She is breathing 6 breaths a minute and her pulse is 58 bpm with poor systematic perfusion. What should you do?

a. Assist ventilations with high flow O2 and transport rapidly
b. Initiate chest compressions and assist ventilations with high flow O2
c. Use an epinephrine auto injector to increase her heart rate
d. Transport with high flow O2 and assist respirations if needed

Question 110: Anaphylaxis may involve more than one of the body's systems. Which of the following systems are involved?

a. Reproductive and respiratory
b. Reproductive and neurological
c. Respiratory and neurological
d. Reproductive and metabolic

Question 111: Your 34 year old patient is breathing on their own at a rate of 18 per minute and an approximate tidal volume of 150 mL. What should you do?

a. Apply a non rebreather mask with high flow O2 at 15 lpm
b. Give positive pressure ventilations with high flow O2
c. Coach your patient to increase their breathing rate
d. Ask the patient if they are having trouble breathing

Question 112: In order to speed delivery of the placenta the EMS provider should?

a. Gently pull on the umbilical cord until it delivers
b. Massage the cervix
c. Position the mother in a prone position
d. Let the placenta deliver on its own

Question 113: Dispatch has reported a man down near a local laundromat. The reporting party says the man is "breathing very fast , but not very deep." The reporting party also says that, "The man has stopped breathing several times, but then begins breathing fast again." What is the most likely cause of this man's respiratory pattern?

a. Somebody hit him in the head with a hammer
b. He is suffering from hyperglycemia
c. An opiate overdose
d. He is drunk

Question 114: You and your partner Tom arrive on scene of a gang shooting where the police have secured the area. There are two patients in their teens with multiple gunshot wounds to the arms, legs, and chest. You would immediately?

a. Treat the most critical patient while Tom watches your back
b. Make sure the police have secured the scene and get a SAMPLE
c. Call for backup and put both patients in the back of your ambulance
d. Apply 3-sided dressing to the chest wounds and assess breathing while your partner treats the other patient

Question 115: When assessing the breathing of an infant or child, you should look for_____?

a. Normal breathing
b. Adequate breathing
c. Presence or absence of breathing
d. Inadequate breathing

Question 116: You and your partner Gene respond to a report of a car vs. pedestrian. An elderly man has been struck by a car and is now on the sidewalk lying supine. Gene takes C-spine and you begin an initial assessment noticing that the man's breathing is fast and very shallow. He does not respond to you and also has some liquid or vomit running from his mouth. The best choice of action would be?

a. Put a C-collar on him and assist ventilations with a BVM and high flow O2
b. Measure and insert an oropharyngeal airway
c. Suction his mouth
d. Do a head tilt chin lift to open his airway

Question 117: A pediatric patient may need additional measures to maintain an open airway. Which of the following is an acceptable method to use?

a. Insert an oral or nasal airway adjunct
b. Place a rolled up towel under the child's neck to align the airway
c. Put the child in a Trendelenburg position on high flow O2 at 15 liters a minute
d. Use Magill forceps to keep the child's tongue from blocking the airway

Question 118: You and your partner Amy arrive on scene to find a woman with hives over much of her body. She is wheezing and complaining of difficulty breathing. Her husband says she was stung by a hornet and has no prior history of allergies. What would be the best course of action?

a. Use an autoinject epinephrine pen and administer to the patient's thigh. Obtain signed transport refusal.
b. Make sure blood pressure is above 100 mmHg and inject her with epinephrine 1/1000.
c. Get her BP, pulse, and respirations and then inject her with epinephrine only if her vitals are within normal limits.
d. High flow O2 and rapid transportation if the patient appears to be going into anaphylaxis.

Question 119: You have a responsive patient who is able to answer your questions. What do you do?

a. History, secondary assessment, vitals
b. Baseline vitals, history, and secondary assessment
c. Secondary assessment, baseline vitals, and history
d. History, vitals, and secondary assessment

Question 120: A call has come in from an indoor amusement park for an allergic reaction. A 16 yr old boy was eating lunch when he ingested a cookie that had small pieces of peanut baked into it. You arrive to find the boy in obvious respiratory stress with swelling and cyanosis around his lips. What would be your best course of action?_____ Why is this boy hypoperfusing?

a. Give High flow O2 attached to a BVM and rapid transport - Urticaria caused his airway to close lowering oxygen levels
b. Inject the patient with epinephrine in the thigh - The high levels of allergen cause the vessels to constrict, impeding transport of O2
c. Assist ventilations via BVM at 12-20 breaths per minute with high flow O2 and rapid transport
d. Give the patient an injection of epinephrine via auto injector - His vasculature is dilated and fluid is leaking from his vessels

Question 121: A 73 year old female was in her backyard gardening when she collapsed to the ground. Her husband told 911 that "she is breathing very fast and will not talk to me." You arrive to find the woman lying on her side in the grass. She is breathing at 7 breaths per minute and her pulse is irregular and very thready. Her lungs also present with crackles upon auscultation As you are taking a blood pressure (88/66) the husband tells you that the woman has been having jaw pain and some weakness for approximately 3 days. What is the most likely cause of this woman's condition and how would you treat her?

a. Hypoperfusion, High flow O2, and transport in Fowler's position
b. Cardiac arrest, Treat for shock, and rapid transport
c. Cardiogenic shock, Assist ventilations, and transport
d. Septic shock, Transport in a position of comfort with high flow O2 via NRB

Question 122: Which of the following patients has adequate respirations?

a. 55 year old woman with paradoxical chest expansion at 22 per minute
b. A 31 year old man breathing at 20 per minute and slightly irregular
c. A 6 month old child who is breathing at 22 per minute
d. A 10 year old who is breathing with accessory muscles at 30 per minute

Question 123: According to the current AHA Guidelines how many milliliters of tidal volume should you deliver via BVM to an adult patient who is apneic?

a. 80ml-100ml
b. 100ml-500ml
c. 500ml-1000ml
d. Just enough to give adequate chest rise

Question 124: If a person has dyspnea what is happening?

a. They are vomiting
b. They are having trouble breathing
c. They cannot breath
d. They are incontinent

Question 125: You are called to a youth summer camp for a 12 year old girl having difficulty breathing. En route to the camp you are told that a group of kids were having lunch when a hive of bees was disturbed near by. The kids took off running and when they stopped the patient began having a hard time breathing. She has no known allergies. What is the best course of action?

a. Verify low blood pressure and then administer epinephrine by auto-injector to the patient's thigh if protocols allow.
b. Ask the girl if she is choking. Initiate treatment and immediate transport in a position of comfort.
c. Apply high flow 02 at 15LPM and assess lung sounds. Place the patient in a position of comfort.
d. Confirm that the patient is not taking any new medications that may have caused the allergic reaction. Apply high flow 02 at 15LPM.

Question 126: A woman with preeclampsia will _____.

a. Have swelling in the feet, hands, and or face
b. Have a dangerously low blood pressure
c. Generally have an uncomplicated birth
d. None of the above

Question 127: You and your partner Steve arrive at an apartment building where you are greeted outside by a very upset woman. She says her husband is upstairs and needs help. He is a 57 year old and was a chain smoker for 35 years. As you enter the apartment, the man is sitting in a tripod position and pursing his lips while exhaling. Why is this patient pursing his lips?

a. So he won't hyperventilate
b. To exhale air quicker
c. He just ate something hot
d. To keep alveoli open with back pressure

Question 128: You arrive on scene at a single-car accident involving a moose. Your patient was driving about 50 MPH when she hit the moose. After completing your scene size up, to which of the following would you proceed?

a. Baseline vitals and oxygen
b. Detailed physical examination
c. The patient's chief complaint
d. SAMPLE history with focused physical examination on c-spine

Question 129: Incident Command has made you transportation officer at a multiple casualty incident. A walking bridge at a nearby park has collapsed and there were 10-20 people on the bridge suffering varying degrees of injuries. You have two hospitals at your disposal. Santa Cruz Hospital is 3 miles away and Valley Hospital is 15 miles away. Which of the following transportation choices would be the BEST?

a. Send all the red tagged patients to Santa Cruz until they are at capacity. Then send any remaining red tagged patients to Valley Hospital followed by yellow and green tagged patients.
b. Send all green tagged patients to Valley Hospital first, followed by the yellow tagged patients until the hospital is at capacity. Once at capacity send all remaining patients to Santa Cruz.
c. Send all red and yellow tagged patients to Valley Hospital, and then send the green and black tagged patients to Santa Cruz Hospital.
d. Send all green tagged patients to Valley Hospital after sending all the red, yellow, and black tagged patients to Santa Cruz.

Question 130: You arrive on scene of a one-car motor vehicle accident. A single female patient can be observed in the car having breathing difficulties. You notice power lines are down across the hood of the car but you do not see any sparks. What would be your best course of action?

a. Get the patient extricated as quickly as possible
b. Notify the power company and keep a safe distance until they have removed the wires
c. Provide assisted ventilations while maintaining c-spine
d. Avoid the wires and begin assessing the patient

Question 131: A person who is in anaphylaxis will have blood vessels that are _____.

a. Constricted
b. Dilated
c. Titrated
d. Clogged

Question 132: You have just delivered a quartet of quadruplets. Q1 has pale blue arms and legs. His pulse is 100 and he is breathing at about 50 breaths per minute. Q2 has a pulse of 130, a respiratory rate of 40, and core cyanosis. Q3 has core cyanosis, a pulse of 60 beats per minute, and a respiratory rate of 30. Q4 is breathing at around 30 breaths per minute. Her pulse is about 110 beats per minute and she has peripheral cyanosis. To which of these children are you going to give CPR?

a. Q1
b. Q2
c. Q3
d. Q4

Question 133: Proper use of an AED should include:

a. Measuring from the corner of the mouth to the earlobe
b. Moistening the pads to ensure electrical conductivity
c. Establishing the patient does not have a pulse
d. Three consecutive shocks

Question 134: You and your partner answer the call for a 1-year-old boy who was dropped on his head by his older brother. His mother said he hit his head on the edge of the coffee table on the way down. You would not expect which of the following?

a. Bruising and hematomas
b. Bleeding between the skull and the scalp
c. Sunken fontanelles
d. Swelling

Question 135: A train derailment has caused two tanker cars to explode and several others to begin leaking an unknown gas. The size of the affected area is large and crosses several county lines. According to NIMS, this type of MCI would benefit most from a:

a. Multiple Command System
b. Unified Command System
c. Singular Command System
d. Coordinated Command System

Question 136: You arrive on scene with your partner Ebstein to find a man in his 50's who is staggering around outside of a casino with blood trickling down his face from a laceration on his head. He complies when you ask him to sit down and he maintains eye contact with you while you ask him questions. You ask him what his name is and he slurs "nibralizxsnafrb". You ask him what day it is and he again slurs "kbmefrolzx". Your partner Ebstein, an expert in linguistics, assures you that what you are hearing is not another language. This patient has a GCS of what?

a. 12

b. 8
c. 14
d. 11

Question 137: You and your partner Monte are transporting a 4 year old child who has ingested some oven cleaner. The mother insists on holding the child during transport. In the best interest of the patient and parent you should?

a. Tell the mother she must get out of the ambulance if you are going to treat her child
b. Explain the reasons quickly why she may not hold the child and secure the child to the stretcher
c. Secure the mother to the stretcher and let her hold the child
d. Seat the mother on the stretcher with the child on her lap and secure the belts around both

Question 138: You are the first EMS unit on scene of a multiple casualty incident. A crane has fallen from a building roof top and ripped through an adjacent building. What should you do according to the ICS?

a. Notify dispatch of the need for an Incident Commander and begin triaging patients.
b. Inform IC of your location and begin triaging patients if the scene is safe.
c. Stay a safe distance from the incident and do what the Incident Commander tells you to do.
d. Take incident command until relieved or reassigned

Question 139: You and your partner Greg are called to a hockey arena where a fan was struck in the side of the chest with a hockey puck that was hit over the protective glass and into the crowd. The man is having a painful time breathing at about 16 a minute. He says his ribs really hurt. What should your treatment include?

a. A chest compression wrap while having the patient maintain his exhaled state
b. High flow O2 via NRB and rapid transport
c. Bag valve mask with oxygen attached
d. Sweeping the tongue out of the way to look for airway obstructions

Question 140: You and your partner whom you have been working with for two years are called to a house where a woman is having chest pain and complaining of shortness of breath. She is diaphoretic and has a pulse of 110, respirations of 22, and a blood pressure of 140/80. She says she has no cardiac or respiratory history. You should?

a. Put her in the ambulance and transport as rapidly as possible
b. Call medical control and ask permission to administer some of her husband's nitro
c. Perform your assessment, put her on O2 at 15 lpm, and transport
d. Get her sample history and try to determine the cause of the respiratory problem

Question 141: Dispatch has called you to the scene of a possible drowning. You and your partner Efron arrive on scene to find two people giving mouth to mouth to a 50ish male. "I am a doctor," announces one of the rescuers, "...he has a good strong pulse but was not breathing when we pulled him from the water." After re-opening the patient's airway and hooking up the bag valve mask, you begin ventilating the patient at _____. Each respiratory cycle should last approximately _____ with a tidal volume of _____.

a. 12-20 breaths per minute / 3-4 seconds / approximately 800ml per breath
b. 10-12 breaths per minute / 5-6 seconds / enough to cause adequate chest rise
c. 20-30 breaths per minute / 2-3 seconds / a large breath
d. 12-20 breaths per minute / 3-4 seconds / approximately 300ml per breath

Question 142: A motor vehicle accident has occurred right in front of your ambulance and requires the patients to be extricated. Your first choice of location to accomplish the rapid extrication should be the?

a. Cut off roof
b. Broken window
c. Open broken windshield
d. The door

Question 143: You are called to the scene of a 35 year old woman in labor. Dispatch tells you that the baby's arm is sticking out of the vagina. You should be prepared to?

a. High flow 02 on the mother, rapid transport, and gently maneuver the baby's arm back into the vagina
b. Gently pull the rest of the baby out by the exposed arm
c. Ask the mother to push and assist with the rest of the delivery
d. Cover the arm and vagina with a moist, sterile dressing and transport rapidly

Question 144: Your patient is a 69 year old female who has a history of diabetes. She is breathing very deeply and very rapidly in a state of respiratory acidosis. Her husband said he woke up to her breathing like this and she would not wake up. You know that this woman is most likely in?

a. Respiratory rebound stage
b. A diabetic coma
c. Diabetic shock
d. Respiratory alkalosis

Question 145: What will Epinephrine do if administered per auto injector?

a. Dilate the bronchial passages and dilate the vessels of the circulatory system
b. Constrict the bronchial passages and dilate the vessels of the circulatory system
c. Dilate the bronchial passages and constrict the vessels of the circulatory system
d. None of the above

Question 146: Without knowing anything else, what condition would you say the following patient is in? A 30 year old male with a pulse rate of 40, breathing at 10 breaths per minute, and a systolic BP of 90.

a. Good
b. Poor
c. Fair
d. Moderate

Question 147: You and your partner Willy have just arrived at a restaurant where a man has fallen through a glass door. He has a laceration across his lower leg approximately 10 inches long and 1.5 inches deep. Which of the following treatment sequences would be the MOST appropriate?

a. Put gloves on - Bandage wound - Pressure to arterial pressure point
b. Apply pressure to the wound - Elevate the legs - Transport
c. Locate and apply pressure to appropriate arterial pressure point - Elevate leg - Transport
d. BSI - Treat patient for shock - Elevate leg

Question 148: Your patient has been kicked in the chest by a horse and is having trouble breathing. Lung sounds are non existent on the right side where she was kicked and you believe she has a tension pneumothorax. During inhalation, her _____ _____ impeding ventilation. When she exhales, her _____ _____.

a. blood pressure rises / blood pressure returns to normal
b. mediastinum moves left / mediastinum shifts, distorting the vena cava which results in poor venous return
c. lung on the affected side takes in air from the pleural space / lung passes that air back into the pleural space which increases intrathorasic pressure
d. ribs over the injured area move outward / ribs move inward over the non injured side

Question 149: Your patient is a 14 year old girl who is complaining of vaginal pain after falling onto the center post of her bike. She is alone and very scared. She has called the accident in on her cell phone and stated that she is bleeding very badly and feeling faint. Besides treating for shock, what other things should you consider with this patient?

a. Transporting in the fowler's position - O2 on nasal canula at 6 lpm
b. Parental release - advice about bike riding
c. If she is having her period - are her parents home
d. Having a female EMT respond for the patient's modesty

Question 150: Gastric distention can interfere with movement of the diaphragm and lead to what other problem?

a. Hypoventilation
b. Hyperglycemia
c. Hyphema
d. Hyperventilation

Question 151: Changes during pregnancy usually include _____.

a. Decrease in blood volume
b. Increased blood pressure
c. Slower heart rate
d. Increase in plasma volume

Question 152: Your patient is the victim of a moderate speed MVA. The patient is unconscious and not breathing. You attempt to open their airway with a jaw thrust maneuver and are unsuccessful. What should you do next?

a. Use the head tilt chin lift maneuver
b. Use the jaw thrust maneuver again
c. Move the patient to a supine position and again attempt to open their airway with the jaw thrust maneuver
d. Put in an OPA and prepare to suction

Question 153: You suspect a significant mechanism of injury. In what order would you conduct the assessment?

a. Vital signs, SAMPLE history, rapid trauma assessment
b. SAMPLE history, rapid trauma assessment, focused physical
c. Primary survey, SAMPLE history, rapid full-body scan
d. Focused trauma, SAMPLE, baseline vitals

Question 154: An unconscious patient would give what type of consent?

a. Implied
b. Expressed
c. Written
d. Verbal

Question 155: You arrive on scene to find an 11 year old girl who was struck by a truck while riding her bike. She is unresponsive to painful stimuli and has a large abrasion on her left side. She is breathing at 24 respirations per minute and regular. Your next course of action would be?

a. C-spine precautions and Administer high flow O2 with an NRB
b. Splint any fractured extremities
c. Start Positive pressure ventilation with a BVM
d. Initiate CPR

Question 156: You are standing by at a local sporting event when a mother rushes up to you with a 3 year old boy in her arms. " He was playing with my car keys and then just started gagging and coughing!", she tells you in a panic. The child is having difficulty breathing and crying along with audible inspiratory stridor. What should you do?

a. Give three quick abdominal thrusts to dislodge the FBAO.
b. Visualize the FBAO and do a finger sweep to remove it.
c. Turn the child upside down and give 3 quick back slaps.
d. Give blow by oxygen and carefully monitor during transport.

Question 157: You arrive on scene with your partner Abe to find a 64 year old woman who is very obese. Her son tells you she has a heart condition. She is unconscious with a baggie of what appears to be street drugs next to her. She is breathing at 18 breaths a minute and they are regular. Her pulse is 99 and her BP is 90/50. What is likely the cause for the low blood pressure?

a. The heart condition
b. The obesity
c. The drugs
d. Her age

Question 158: Anatomical differences in a child's respiratory system can make opening and maintaining the airway a difficult and challenging process. Which of the following choices correctly states some of the problems and solutions associated with these anatomical differences?

a. A child's larynx sits more posterior and superior in the throat making it easier for the tongue to fall back and block the trachea. Putting a rolled up towel under the child's head can help align the oropharynx and trachea which will assist in ventilations.
b. A child's pharynx is larger in proportion to that of an adult's and is easily blocked by swelling or mucous. Using a Nasopharyngeal will assist in passing these blockages and making the airway patent.
c. A child's tongue is larger and takes up considerably more room in the mouth. Using a tongue depressor to hold the tongue down while inserting an OPA without rotating it will be more effective than techniques used in adults.
d. A child's cricoid cartilage is larger and less flexible than that of an adult making it more susceptible to blockage. Using a flexible or french catheter to suction the cricoid opening will aid in making the airway patent.

Question 159: You have just arrived on scene with your partner Ellen to a call. It's a 75 year old man with chest pain. He has already taken 1 nitro tablet, but the pain persists. What should you do?

a. Make sure the nitro is his and that it hasn't passed it's expiration date and give him another one
b. Make sure his BP is under 100 and if so give him another nitro
c. Withhold oxygen until you get a BP and then administer 1 nitro
d. Ask him if he takes any erectile dysfunction drugs and take his BP

Question 160: It is the middle of winter and you and your partner are called to the scene of a homeless man having breathing problems. You arrive to find him laying on a sidewalk on a calm, but very cold night. He is likely losing heat from?

a. Conduction
b. Convection
c. Refraction
d. Evaporation

Question 161: Which of the following is considered a sign?

a. The patient states they are dizzy
b. There is blood in the vomit of the patient
c. The patient says they took their insulin
d. The patient states they have a headache

Question 162: Which of the following would be the best indication that a patient is suffering from hypoxia?

a. They are breathing shallow and fast
b. Their oxygen saturation is 87% while you have them on O2 at 15 LPM
c. They are cool and moist
d. Their pulse is rapid and their skin is pale

Question 163: You arrive on scene to find a woman in her 20's who phoned in her own diabetic emergency. She is now unconscious and breathing at 20 a minute with a pulse of 110. She told the dispatcher on the phone that she had hypoglycemia and had not eaten that day. Your best course of treatment would include?

a. A ham sandwich and soda
b. 1-2 tubes of glucose orally until she feels better
c. ARGAD if accessible
d. Obtain a blood sugar, O2 via NRB at 15 lpm, and Initiate an IV of D5W

Question 164: You are assessing a patient who is complaining of severe chest pain. They are sweating and their BP is 96/55. You have their medications with you and they include a prescription for nitroglycerin. You contact medical control and they order you to give the patient 1 nitro tablet sublingually. What would you do?

a. Repeat the blood pressure and ask again what they would like you to do
b. Give the patient 1 nitro tablet as instructed
c. Instruct medical control to get out their protocol books and look under contraindications for nitro administration
d. None of the above

Question 165: You are transporting an unconscious but breathing 55 year old male who has suffered a head injury. He has an oropharyngeal airway in place. You hear gurgling sounds during his respirations and you need to suction his airway. How should this be accomplished?

a. With a flexible catheter/on the way out
b. By inserting the catheter to just below the vocal chords and then initiating suction
c. By inserting the catheter and suctioning until the airway is clear
d. 15 seconds/on the way in
By inserting the catheter for 15 seconds only and suctioning on the way in

Question 166: A child between 3-5 would have normal vitals if they were?

a. 35 breaths a minute, pulse of 88, and Systolic BP of 100
b. 24 breaths a minute, pulse of 76, and Systolic BP of 98
c. 20 breaths a minute, pulse of 120, and Systolic BP of 120
d. 20 breaths a minute, pulse of 100, and Systolic BP of 110

Question 167: A 45 year old male patient is complaining of headaches and fatigue. He has had a fever of over 102 degrees for 3 days now and he says his neck hurts when he moves his head around. These signs and symptoms make you consider that this man is suffering from?

a. A mild stroke
b. Migraine headache
c. Meningitis
d. Cerebral aneurism

Question 168: You and your partner Mark arrive on scene to find a 35 year old man who is slurring his speech. He shows positive for left arm drift and the left side of his face is drooping slightly when he tries to speak. How should this patient be transported?

a. On their left side
b. In Fowler's
c. Trendelenburg
d. On their right side

Question 169: You are the Incident Commander at the scene of a bus rollover. A tourist group of approximately 25 senior citizens was on the bus when it overturned on a sharp corner. Which of the following actions would be appropriate?

a. Help with extrication of the patients from the bus and set up a triage area
b. Call for fire suppression from the fire department and traffic control from law enforcement, then establish a red zone
c. Assigning a triage officer, treatment officer, and a transportation officer
d. None of the actions would be appropriate

Question 170: You and your partner Rob arrive on scene to find a woman in her 37th week of pregnancy. She says that she feels like she is ready to give birth and asks you to take her to the hospital. While Rob takes vital signs in route, you are assessing how far along the woman is. She has some hemorrhaging from the vaginal opening which makes you think that she may have _____ or _____.

a. Twins or triplets
b. A premature delivery or prolapsed umbilical cord

c. Placenta previa or placenta abruptio
d. Had abdominal trauma

Question 171: Which of the following is a high priority condition?

a. Child birth
b. Severe pain
c. Controlled bleeding of the wrists
d. An adult breathing at 20 a minute

Question 172: You are assessing an 83 year old woman who has COPD and CHF. She is sitting upright in her chair and appears to understand that you are an EMT here to help her. You should?

a. Never break eye contact
b. Call the patient something endearing like honey
c. Be honest with the patient about her conditions
d. Stand in front of her to facilitate communication

Question 173: Nitroglycerin has what affect on the body's vessels?

a. Dilation to ease the preload on heart
b. Contraction to ease workload on heart
c. Removes fluid from the lungs
d. Slows down the breathing to ease the patient's pain

Question 174: Which breath sounds would you likely hear from a person whose alveoli contain fluid?

a. Crackles
b. Wheezes
c. Cheyne-Stokes
d. Bilateral

Question 175: With regard to the airway and breathing of a child, which of the following statements is most accurate?

a. You should role up a towel to 1 inch thick and place it under the child's neck when in need of assisting ventilations
b. Airway adjuncts should not be used in children as a child's airway is not shaped as an adults
c. Use of a pediatric resuscitation tape can aid in the selection of the correct equipment
d. A child who is breathing adequately will use accessory muscles

Question 176: Which of the following is a rare cause of respiratory failure in children?

a. Upper airway obstruction
b. Epiglottitis
c. Anaphylaxis
d. Croup

Question 177: Your patient is an 86 year old female who is complaining of difficulty breathing. She says it has been getting worse for the last few hours. She has a cough that she says, "has been..(breath) a companion(breath) for years." During your assessment you find that she has a rapid pulse and diminished breath sounds on her right side. She also says her chest hurts every time she coughs. What is the likely cause of this woman's complaint?

a. COPD
b. Pneumothorax
c. Pulmonary Effusions
d. Anaphylaxis

Question 178: Using lights and sirens during a cardiac arrest transport is?

a. Mandated by the DOT
b. Not necessary
c. A consideration for moving quickly and safely through traffic
d. A good way to calm the patient

Question 179: You and your partner Naven have just arrived at a home where a woman in her 70's was reported to have passed out. You enter the residence to find a man in his 20's performing rescue breathing on the elderly woman who is supine on the floor. Naven attaches the AED and advises the man to move away. He pushes the analyze button and no shock is advised. The two of you begin CPR, delivering approximately_____. After 1 cycle of CPR an elderly gentleman enters the room and shows you a valid looking DNR signed by the patient and her doctor. What should you do?_____

a. 12 breaths and 200 compressions over 2 minutes / Call medical control and ask for guidance
b. 6 breaths and 110 compressions over 1 minute / Respect the DNR
c. 12 to 20 breaths and 100 compressions over 1 minute / Respect the DNR
d. 6 breaths and 100 compressions per minute / Contact the signing doctor to verify authenticity

Question 180: An intervention for someone who is apneic would be _____.

a. The use of an oropharyngeal
b. The use of assisted ventilations
c. Manually opening the airway
d. All of the above

Question 181: You and your partner Loni arrive on scene to find 4 patients. Which one of them would be your priority?

a. A 54 year old man complaining of chest pain with a BP of 130/80 and a pain severity rating of 4
b. A 17 year old with a systolic BP of 102 mm Hg
c. A 7 year old who is conscious, with respirations of 27, and a systolic of 68 mm Hg
d. A 46 year old female with a broken ankle and a broken tibia

Question 182: The National Incident Management System (NIMS) includes a componant referred to as "Interoperability". This componant is concerned with:

a. Inter-agency communications before, during and after an MCI.
b. The immediate establishment of Incident Command.
c. Communication between EMS, fire and law enforcement during an MCI.
d. How EMS units operate as a team when communications are down.

Question 183: You are dispatched to a report of a breathing difficulty. Upon arrival, you find a 67 year old female patient who appears to be tired, but responds to your questioning. Her husband reports that she appeared to have trouble breathing when he came home. She reports that she has been progressively becoming more short of breath as the day has progressed. She has a history of breast cancer and a fractured left tibia. You assess her vitals and they reveal a blood pressure of 68/50, pulse of 80, and respiratory rate of 32. Her oxygen saturation is 79% on her home cannula at 2 lpm. Your next step in the care of this patient should include?

a. High flow oxygen via NRB, consider rapid transport
b. Increase her flow rate of her cannula to 6 lpm and package the patient for transport
c. Allow patient to sign a patient refusal
d. High flow oxygen via NRB and wait to see if her oxygen saturation increases

Question 184: The structure of an incident command system:

a. Is broken down by the degree of distress or trauma associated with the event
b. Can contain multiple sectors, but only one incident commander
c. Is decided at the scene by the safety officer
d. Is not effective at organizing agencies from different areas

Question 185: Which patient is most viable?

a. 9 month old infant found apneic, pulseless, cool, blue, and stiff after nap.
b. 96 y/o female with a valid DNR who is not breathing, but has a pulse of 38.
c. 38 y/o male who has had both legs torn off from a railway incident. He has agonal respirations, and no palpable pulse.
d. 5 y/o who fell through the ice and was submerged for 10 minutes before being brought to your ambulance. She is not breathing and doesn't have a pulse.

Question 186: What is the area of hazardous contamination known as?

a. Green zone
b. Yellow zone
c. Hot zone
d. Black zone

Question 187: After applying a cervical collar to a patient and securing them to the backboard what must you check before transporting them?

a. That you have enough responders to lift the patient
b. Their CMS
c. That the stretcher is low enough to load them on
d. Proper spinal alignment

Question 188: You arrive on scene with your partner to a call of "man down". You pull into the driveway of the house in a very exclusive part of town. In the driveway a man is lying face up with his eyes closed. After making sure the scene is safe, what actions will help you gather the most information in the shortest period of time?

a. Check his pulse with your hand and look at his nose for flaring
b. Start bagging him with high flow O2 and supplemental oxygen
c. Look for the responsible party and question them about the events then put the AED on the patient
d. Check his pulse with your hand while you put your ear near his mouth and look down at the sternum for chest rise

Question 189: You are called to a scene of a 3-year-old who is not breathing and is pulseless. Your CPR should include compressions at what depth?

a. 1-2 inches
b. 1.5-2.5 inches
c. At least 1/3rd the depth of the chest
d. No compressions, it's a child

Question 190: You arrive on scene with your partner Leonard to the report of a child appearing lethargic. Upon entering the house, you see a 9-year-old girl lying on the couch. Her father says she has been breathing strangely and began vomiting about 45 minutes ago. During your assessment, you determine she needs to be transported to the ER immediately. Which of the following sets of vitals would lead you to believe this girl is in need of immediate transport?

a. BP 104/60, respirations of 24 per minute and a pulse of 82
b. BP 100/58, respirations of 14 per minute and a pulse of 130
c. BP 108/64, respirations of 20 per minute and a pulse of 100
d. BP 116/70, respirations of 27 per minute and a pulse of 96

Question 191: During one person CPR you can assess ventilations by watching what?

a. Bilateral rise and fall of the chest
b. Their capillary refill
c. Nostril flare
d. The patient's blood pressure

Question 192: You are called to a neighborhood pool where a 5 year old girl was found floating unconscious. She is cyanotic and has no muscle tone. Your partner Greg does not find a pulse and the child is not breathing. Your CPR should include a compression to ventilation ratio of_____ and each compression should be at a depth of_____.

a. 15:2 / one third to one half the depth of the chest
b. 15:2 / one third of the anterior-posterior diameter of the chest
c. 30:2 / 1.5 to 2 inches in depth
d. 15:2 / just enough to give adequate chest rise

Question 193: Why would inserting a suction catheter into the mouth with the suction active be incorrect?

a. You were not taught to do it that way
b. You may cause the patient to aspirate the contents of the mouth
c. It depletes the patient's oxygen supply
d. Big chunks are often at the top and will clog the suction before you get deep enough

Question 194: You are driving an ambulance with lights and sirens going when you approach a busy 4 way stop. The car stopped to your right appears to acknowledge that your ambulance is responding to an emergency. As you continue through the intersection the car pulls out in front of you and you collide with the driver's side door. Who is at fault and why?

a. You the ambulance driver is at fault because you did not stop, slow down or use due regard at the intersection
b. The driver of the car is at fault as the emergency vehicle gave proper warning and has the right of way privilege in all states
c. You the ambulance driver is at fault as you should have given the car on your right the right of way by law

d. The driver of the car is at fault as he/she pulled in front of your emergency vehicle while moving through the intersection

Question 195: Which type of shock would you suspect to find in a patient who has vomiting, urinating, and diarrhea?

a. Anaphylactic shock
b. Neurogenic shock
c. Septic shock
d. Hypovolemic shock

Question 196: Two ambulances are proceeding together toward a scene and are approaching an intersection where the traffic light is currently green. You are the driver of the second ambulance. Which of the following choices describes the best method for proceeding through the intersection?

a. use the same siren tone as the first ambulance as a different tone may cause other cars and pedestrians to believe there are two emergency vehicles approaching from two different directions.
b. turn off your sirens until you have cleared the intersection. The siren on the first ambulance is adequate if you are moving together and will be less likely to frighten other drivers.
c. drive side by side with the first ambulance occuping both lanes through the intersection. This will help prevent other drivers from "leaching" and using you to move through traffic.
d. use a different siren tone than the one the first ambulance is using and consider slowing down to look for pedestrians or other cars as the light may change.

Question 197: You have responded to a request for transportation of a female patient in her 37th week of pregnancy. You arrive to find the woman in active labor with contractions less than 2 minutes apart. The baby is crowning. What are you going to do?

a. BSI, Apply gentle, supportive pressure to the baby's head and mother's perineum to prevent explosive delivery. Check for nucal cord as the head emerges. Suction the baby's mouth and then nose. Guide the baby's head downward to facilitate delivery of the first shoulder and then upward to deliver the other shoulder.
b. BSI, Apply gentle, direct pressure to the fontanelle to prevent explosive delivery. As the head delivers, suction the nose first and then the mouth. Check to see if the cord is wrapped around the baby's neck. Gently guide the baby's head upward to assist in delivery of the first shoulder and then downward to get the other shoulder to emerge.
c. BSI, Wait for the baby's head to fully emerge from the vagina and then suction the nose and then mouth for no more than 5 seconds. Check for nucal cord and if it exists, try to gently slip the cord over the baby's head. Gently guide the baby's head downward to assist in delivering the lower shoulder then gently upward to facilitate delivering the upper shoulder.
d. BSI, Ensure the umbilical cord is not wrapped around the baby's neck. Suction the mouth and then nose and coach the mother to push during each contraction. As the shoulders emerge and the baby is completely delivered, clamp the cord at the baby's umbilicus and cut approximately 4 to 6 inches away from the clamp with a sterile pair of scissors or a surgical scalpel.

Question 198: Your patient is a 2-year-old child. He is in respiratory distress and you have identified the need for oxygen therapy. Why have you chosen blow-by oxygen for this patient?

a. The National Standards say to use blow-by oxygen for all children that are 2.
b. It is possible the child is choking and you shouldn't place a mask over the face of a choking victim.
c. He is probably frightened and will tolerate oxygen near him, but not a mask directly placed on his face.
d. Blow-by oxygen provides the highest concentration of oxygen that you can deliver.

Question 199: The primary survey is used to:

a. Get a rapid understanding of the scene
b. Gather vital signs and discover injuries
c. Gather history of the event
d. Rapidly identify critical patients and life threatening conditions

Question 200: While talking with a group of daycare children you notice a child who seems to be having an increased work of breathing. Which of the following signs helped you come to this decision?

a. Head bobbing
b. Dilated pupils
c. Goose bumps
d. Red, flushed skin

Question 201: Driving an ambulance fast?

a. Increases chances of patient survival
b. Increases the stopping distance
c. Increases response efficiency
d. Decreases the velocity

Question 202: You arrive on scene with your partner Dale to find a woman in respiratory distress. She is walking around with her hands up in the air and you can hear audible wheezing on inspiration. Bystanders tell you that she was eating a hot dog when she started choking. It has been 10 minutes since she started having breathing difficulties. The best course of action would be?

a. Heimlich maneuver
b. Transport and encourage her to cough
c. Wait until she passes out from choking then do chest compressions
d. Encourage her to cough and have a family member sign a PCR

Question 203: An adult with a respiration rate of _____per minute would be considered within normal limits. A child aged 3-5 with a respiration rate of_____per minute would be considered within normal limits and an infant who is breathing at_____per minute would be considered within normal limits.

a. 22, 32, 42
b. 11, 6, 15
c. 20, 40, 60
d. 16, 25, 40

Question 204: Your patient is a 75 year old male who may have had a stroke. He is unconscious and breathing with snoring respirations. After performing a head tilt chin lift maneuver, the snoring is still present. What is your best course of action?

a. Suction the patient's mouth and nose, removing the secretions that are likely causing the snoring sounds
b. Try the jaw thrust maneuver
c. Insert a nasopharyngeal, measured from the nostril to the earlobe
d. Insert an oropharyngeal, measured from the earlobe to the chin

Question 205: You are dispatched to the call of a woman with a severe stomach ache. When you arrive on scene you find her doubled over in pain lying on the floor of the bathroom. There is vomit in the toilet and your patient is complaining that she is going to vomit again. She denies falling or having any pain anywhere but her stomach. Assessing her abdomen you find it to be very tender to the touch and she pulls away when you palpate only 1/2 inch deep. What other signs and symptoms might you find with this patient?

a. Tachycardia - hypotension - fever
b. Bottle of poison - cyanosis, and crepitus
c. Broken ribs - hypertension, and deep rapid breathing
d. Rebound tenderness - metabolic acidosis

Question 206: You and your partner Duval arrive on scene to find a woman who has suffered a blunt trauma to the chest from a swing on a carnival ride. She is having difficulty breathing and upon auscultation you hear nothing on the right side. This woman likely has a_____ and would be suffering from_____as the collapsed lung is incapable of oxygenating any blood.

a. Flail chest / hyperventilation
b. Pneumothorax / hypoxia
c. Hemoptysis / hypoventilation
d. Broken jaw /severe pain

Question 207: You and your partner Sue have just arrived on scene to an unknown injury/ illness. You see a man lying against the side of a convenience store who appears unconscious. One of the witnesses tells you that the man was standing there and then just fell over hitting his head on the building and sliding down into the sitting position. As you check his pulse and respirations you find that he is breathing shallow at about 10 per minute, and his pulse is rapid. What would you do first for this patient?

a. Pinch his shoulder to see if he wakes up and then get a BP
b. Question the witnesses to see if someone really hit him
c. Do a focused trauma assessment and then take his blood pressure
d. Maintain c spine and move him to a supine position, then open his airway

Question 208: Respirations in an adolescent would be considered normal at _____.

a. 16 breaths per minute
b. 24 breaths per minute
c. 32 breaths per minute
d. 35 breaths per minute

Question 209: You arrive on scene with your partner Emilio to find a woman who is having problems breathing. She is speaking in 1 or 2 word bursts and is on oxygen at 3 liters per minute. There is an ashtray next to her bed loaded with cigarette butts. She says her care taker called the ambulance and she does not want you there. She says she will allow you to take her vitals but then you have to leave. Her BP is 100/60 her pulse is 48 and her respirations are 18. She says she is 89 years old and has a pacemaker and is on high blood pressure medication. "I just want to be old, please leave", she says. What should you do?

a. Transport her to the ER. Her vitals dictate that you must
b. Tell the care giver to quit calling and giving false alarms
c. Respect her wishes and leave, asking her to please call if she needs medical attention
d. Prepare to bag her and transport when she eventually passes out

Question 210: Which of the following would be a sign that CPR may not be necessary?

a. Stiff neck and jaw
b. Core cyanosis
c. No pulse or respirations
d. The patient is unconscious

Question 211: The heart muscle has the ability to contract without neural stimulation. This is called?

a. Automaticity
b. Contractility
c. Autonetronic
d. Diastole

Question 212: You and your partner Ebstein have been summoned to a residence where a 53 yr old woman has had a syncopic episode. You arrive to find her sitting on the couch sipping a glass of water. She states that she is feeling perfectly fine now. At this time a teenage girl enters the room with a monster mask in her hand. She tells you that she frightened her mother while wearing the mask. After administering oxygen to this patient, what would be the best course of action?_____What was most likely the cause of this woman's hypoperfusion?_____

a. Do a focused physical exam on whatever injuries she has. Neurogenic shock is caused by pump failure to properly oxygenate the brain
b. Have her lay down for a while until her blood pressure is back to normal. Increased vasoconstriction during the fight or flight response causes the body to shunt blood away from the brain
c. Do a rapid trauma assessment to make sure she was not injured in the fall. Her sympathetic nervous system caused widespread vasodilation
d. Help her to the ambulance for transport and evaluation at the hospital. Her nervous system reacted to the scare by increasing vascular pressure, impairing oxygen transport

Question 213: You are responding to the scene of a two car collision which will require you to drive on the state highway for approximately 10 miles and then exit on the right side where you will drive an additonal 1.5 miles to the scene. Which of the following answer choices would be the most proper way of doing this?

a. As you approach the onramp to the highway use only your emergency lights and not your sirens. Travel in the right hand lane for 10 miles and then exit to the off ramp. Turn sirens back on and continue to scene
b. Before you enter the highway turn off your lights and sirens. Move to the far left or "passing lane" and then turn lights and sirens back on. As you approach the exit turn lights and sirens off again and move to the off ramp. Once on the off ramp turn lights and sirens back on.
c. Enter the highway and move to the left lane. Turn off sirens and lights and continue the 10 miles to the exit ramp. Turn lights and sirens back on and then exit the highway to the off ramp and continue to the scene.
d. Enter the highway without lights and sirens and continue in the right lane for 10 miles. Turn lights and sirens on and exit the highway on to the off ramp and continue to the scene.

Question 214: Asthma is classified into two types.

a. Infection asthma, which is caused by a cold or flu and is usually seen in children rather than adults. Irritant asthma is more common in adults and involves chemicals or air pollution as the contributing cause of the narrowed bronchioles
b. Extrinsic asthma, which is more common in childhood, causes brochioles constriction as a result of an outside substance like dust. Intrinsic asthma is more common in adults where no specific cause for the bronchioles constriction can be identified

c. Allergen induced asthma, which is more common in adults than children, can be triggered by pet dander. Exercise induced asthma can be caused by rapid breathing in cold air which causes a narrowing of the bronchioles

d. Drug based asthma is triggered by narcotics such as cocaine or other inhaleable substances used recreationally. Food based asthma is more often associated with adults and is most often caused by seafood or nut allergies that progress into asthma causing brochospasms

Question 215: You and your partner Benji are called to an apartment complex for an 82 year old woman experiencing chest pain. You recognize the address as one that you have been to several times in the past few months. You enter the apartment to find the woman pale and diaphoretic. She has a BP of 198/99 and she is breathing at 20 breaths per minute. Which part of your assessment will determine her treatment?

a. Oxygen saturation and difficulty breathing
b. OPQRST and SAMPLE
c. Rapid trauma assessment and treatment for shock
d. Determining known allergies and medications

Question 216: The pediatric assessment triangle is composed of three elements:

a. Level of Consciousness, Quality of Respirations, General Appearance
b. Muscle Tone, Respiratory depth and rate, Perfusion
c. Circulation, Appearance, Work of Breathing
d. Blood pressure, Pulse rate, Respiratory Rate

Question 217: Which of the following would be considered a priority patient?

a. A pregnant patient who is having contractions 15 minutes apart
b. A 24 year old male who has a broken tibia
c. A 55 year old female who has a blood pressure of 178/90
d. A 34 year old man who was stung by several bees

Question 218: You and your partner Bob are just pulling up to a call for a man down with CPR in progress. Dispatch has told you that the man has an extensive cardiac history and had just finished golfing with friends when he collapsed in the parking lot. According to the AHA which of the sequences is most correct?

a. Turns on AED power, Attaches AED to the patient, Check pulse and Initiate analysis of the rhythm
b. BSI, Briefly question rescuers about arrest events, Analyze rhythm, Check pulse
c. BSI, Check pulse, Begin compressions, Open airway
d. BSI, Check pulse, Open airway, Begin compressions,

Question 219: What is dependant lividity?

a. The dependence of a person on another to live
b. The anger associated with a head injury
c. Blood settling at the lowest point in the body and visible through the skin
d. The stretch associated with the pericardium during diastolic contraction

Question 220: You arrive on scene to find a 101 year old woman who is sitting in a wheelchair smoking a cigarette. Her eyes are closed but she opens them when she hears you come into the room. You ask her name, she seems confused. You ask her to reach out and grab your hand, she does without hesitation. This woman has a GCS of what?

a. 12
b. 10
c. 14
d. 15

Question 221: The patient is a 6 year old girl whose mother says has been sick for a few days and then started having breathing problems this morning. Upon assessment, you notice the child is flaring her nostrils and has a hoarse voice when talking. What is she most likely suffering from and what should you do?

a. She could have croup and needs to be transported with a nasal cannula at 4 lpm
b. She could have tonsillitis and will require transport to the hospital in a position of comfort
c. She could have epiglottitis and needs to be transported with high flow O2 on an NRB
d. She could have SARS and should be transported wearing a HEPA mask

Question 222: Your patient is an unresponsive 44 year old female who has a pulse but is not breathing. How should you proceed with CPR?

a. Immediate chest compressions followed by two rescue breaths
b. 2 quick rescue breaths and then provide 10-12 breaths per minute
c. 2 quick rescue breaths and 12-20 breaths per minute
d. Attach the AED and analyze, then begin CPR

Question 223: What should be done to a French tip catheter after suctioning a patient's airway?

a. Throw it away
b. Flush with sterile water in preparation for additional suctioning
c. Put it in the sharps container
d. Take it home for your kids to play with

Question 224: You assess a young man who has yellow colored sclera. You would suspect he is suffering from?

a. Kidney disease
b. Hephaltic failure
c. Pancreatic maltosis
d. Liver failure

Question 225: What is a primary cause of abdominal pain and tenderness upon palpation?

a. Acute pericardial irritation
b. Fecal leakage into the pleural space
c. Rupture of the gastrointestinal tract
d. Blood in the retroperitoneal space

Question 226: During anaphylactic shock, the patient's BP is likely to _____.

a. Increase
b. Decrease
c. Stay the same
d. Be tachycardic

Question 227: There are two separate respiratory drives. The _____ and the _____. If a COPD patient is a carbon dioxide retainer then_____

a. Hypoxic / Carbon dioxide / You should deliver oxygen via nasal canula at 4-6 LPM
b. Autonomic / Protonomic / You should deliver oxygen via NRB at 12-15 LPM
c. Carbon monoxide / Hypoxic / You should not deliver oxygen as it will inhibit the patient's hypoxic drive
d. Pneumonic / Pleuritic / Only humidified oxygen should be delivered. Non humidified O2 will cause the alveoli to stick together

Question 228: Who decides what the minimum data set is for a PCR?

a. OSHA
b. ADC
c. NEMSES
d. NIMDA

Question 229: You are treating a patient who is complaining of chest pain. They are diaphoretic with a blood pressure of 98/50. You have their medications on board which include a prescription for nitroglycerin. Medical control has instructed you to administer 1 nitroglycerin tablet sublingually. How would you respond?

a. Respectfully disagree and state that you feel it is in the best interest of the patient with a blood pressure so low to not lower it any further by administering nitroglycerin
b. Administer 1 nitroglycerin tablet as instructed
c. Instruct medical control to get out their protocol books and look under contraindications for nitroglycerin administration
d. Repeat the vital signs to medical control and ask if they still wish to have you administer the nitroglycerin with the blood pressure that low.

Question 230: A 5 year old boy has fallen down the stairs at a daycare. You have responded with your partner Oli. Utilizing the PAT, what would you use to rapidly form a general impression of this patient?

a. Your eyes and ears
b. A rapid trauma assessment and SAMPLE history
c. Stethoscope and BP cuff
d. The level of distress of the parent

Question 231: 911 dispatch calls you to the scene of a "man down". You arrive to find a man sitting up against the wall of his garage. He has a glazed look in his eyes and abnormal respirations. The breaths begin slow and shallow and then gradually get faster and deeper. The rate and depth then decrease to the point of apnea. What do you suspect is wrong with this patient? What are you going to do for them?

a. They are hypoglycemic/ Give oral glucose
b. They are intoxicated / Make sure they have a ride home
c. They are hyperglycemic / Rapid transport to the ER

d. They had a stroke / Give high flow oxygen

Question 232: Dispatch has called your unit to an MVA involving a city bus and a minivan. The driver of the minivan plowed into the side of the bus as it was stopping to pick up passengers. Everyone on the bus is fine, but the driver of the minivan is having difficulty breathing. His pulse rate is very rapid and his jugular veins are bulging. His trachea has shifted from the midline and his skin is cool and pale. He is complaining of severe chest pain and has a bottle of nitro clutched in his hand. What is likely wrong with this man, and what is considered proper treatment?

a. This man likely suffered a heart attack before hitting the bus. After taking his blood pressure, administer 1 nitro if the systolic pressure is above 100 mmHg
b. This man likely has a tension pneumothorax caused by impact to the steering wheel. Treatment would include performing a needle thoracentesis
c. This man is likely suffering from a dissected aorta. Treatment would include C-spine precautions and rapid transport with high flow O2
d. This man likely has a pleural effusion from a pre-existing condition. Treatment would include administration of a diuretic

Question 233: You arrive on scene with your partner to a restaurant where a man was reported to be choking. You enter and find an unconscious cyanotic male on the floor. He is supine with BBQ sauce on his mouth and a napkin in his hand. What would you do for this patient?

a. Verify apnea, give two slow breaths with high flow O2, and administer back thrusts until the object has been removed.
b. Ask the bystanders what happened. Verify no pulse, and attach the AED. Tell everyone to stand back, and hit analyze, following the prompts.
c. Administer abdominal thrusts, followed by a finger sweep, and then administer high flow O2. Monitor patient while transporting.
d. Head tilt, chin lift, verify apnea and begin Compressions. Upon completion of the compressions, give two slow breaths looking for chest rise and fall.

Question 234: Cheyne-Stokes breathing is characterized by _____.

a. Uneven breaths with periods of apnea
b. Deep rapid breaths
c. Bradypnea
d. Rapid breathing very shallow

Question 235: You have an unconscious patient. What do you do?

a. Start CPR immediately
b. Baseline vitals, primary assessment, and secondary assessment
c. ABCs, History taking, Rapid full body scan
d. ABC, Baseline vitals, Transport decision

Question 236: The Incident Command System (ICS) is used to:

a. Ensure efficient use of resources, public and responder safety as well as the successful completion of incident management goals.
b. Ensure that responses to MCI's are rapid, organized and well managed.
c. Prevent individual agencies from making poor response decisions because of poor communications or lack of resources.
d. Create organizational goals for NIMS during natural disasters, terrorist acts or Hazmat incidents.

Question 237: You and your partner Toby arrive at a motel in response to a 911 call for an unconscious female. You find the woman pulseless and while Toby hooks up the AED, you begin delivering compressions. How many compressions per minute would you give this woman?

a. 60-80 compressions per minute
b. 100-109 compressions per minute
c. 150 compressions per minute
d. 90-100 compressions per minute

Question 238: You arrive on scene with your partner Aaron to a call of an unknown injury/ illness. You pull into the driveway of an apartment building. In the parking area is a woman lying face up with her eyes closed. After making sure the scene is safe, what would be the most efficient means for gathering useful information on this patient?

a. Check her pulse with your hand - look at her nose for flaring
b. Check her pulse with your hand while you put your ear near her mouth and look down the sternum for chest rise
c. Look for the person that reported the call and question them about the event
d. Start bagging her with high flow O2

Question 239: Incident Command has put you in charge of setting up the landing zone for a helicopter transport. What size area will you try to procure for this zone? What is the minimum acceptable size for this zone?

a. 500 ft X 500 ft / minimum of 250 feet X 250 feet
b. 100 feet X 100 feet / minimum of 60 feet X 60 feet
c. 50 feet X 50 feet / minimum of 25 feet X 25 feet
d. 25 feet X 25 feet / minimum of 15 feet by 15 feet

Question 240: A child is breathing at 32 breaths per minute. This would be considered _____.

a. In range
b. Above range
c. Below range
d. Bradypneic

Question 241: Chest compressions on a newborn that is not breathing adequately should be done at what depth?

a. 1/4 inch
b. about 1/3 to 1/2 the depth of the chest
c. 1 inch
d. 1.25 inch

Question 242: A 4 year old boy has fallen from a swing and landed on his side. He is complaining of stomach pain. Which of the following assessment techniques would not be utilized to determine if this child is going into shock?

a. Taking his pulse
b. Assessing his breathing
c. Assessing his skin circulation
d. Taking his blood pressure

Question 243: A freight car has overturned and is spilling hundreds of gallons of hazardous chemicals into a local creek. Incident Command has told you that the toxicity of the hazardous material is a level 3. What level of protection must any personnel entering this area be wearing?

a. Level 1 protection
b. Level C protection
c. Level D protection
d. Level A or B protection

Question 244: You and your partner Obi have been dispatched to a home for breathing difficulties. You arrive to find a 50 year old man in bed with labored breathing. His respiration rate is 20 with only very slight chest rise. His color is slightly pale and his pulse is weak. Family members tell you that the man has AIDS. When this history is presented Obi says, " I am sorry, but I don't want to catch AIDS. I can't help". Obi then leaves the house. What has just occurred?

a. Obi has abandoned the patient by refusing to administer care. He has a duty to act
b. A breakdown in communication between you and Obi has compromised the trust of the family and patient in EMS
c. Obi has correctly determined that the scene is not safe and removed himself from the environment
d. Obi has caused psychological damage to the family. Physical harm to the patient is likely without his assistance

Question 245: You and your partner Nick are dispatched to the scene of a small building fire, just as backup and possible rehabilitation. As you round a corner near the scene, you see 10-12 people lying in a yard a few houses away from the fire. Some are in obvious distress and others are walking aimlessly down the street.. Which of the following choices would be the most appropriate for you and Nick to take?

a. Do a rapid visual triage of the wounded and begin treating those with the worst injuries
b. Call dispatch and request traffic control for the street in front of the building. After law enforcement has the street secure begin triaging the patients
c. Go to the building as dispatched and report to the IC
d. Contact the IC and notify them of the current situation, triage and order more resources through command

Question 246: You have just arrived on scene to a call of man down. A man is lying prone on the sidewalk outside of a bar and there are several bystanders who say they witnessed him just fall over forward. As you check his pulse and respirations you find that he is breathing shallow at about 8 per minute and his pulse is 112. What would be the proper choice of action?

a. Shake him to see if he wakes up, take his blood pressure, and put a c-collar on him
b. While maintaining c-spine precautions log roll him to a supine position and open his airway
c. Do a rapid trauma assessment and then take his blood pressure
d. Ask the bystanders if he had been drinking and then log roll him onto a backboard

Question 247: You arrive on scene at a local park for a reported drug overdose. A man in his 30's, pale, with an obvious altered LOC comes stumbling toward you and your partner. He mumbles something unintelligible and then lies down in front of you in a supine position. His respirations are of normal depth, but the rate is a little bit fast. He has a fixed gaze, straight up, and he continues mumbling something about "His sister and a hamburger". A quick check of his pulse reveals he is tachycardic and you note his skin is moist. A blood pressure reading shows 138/82. What is most likely wrong with this man and what would be the most appropriate course of treatment?

a. He has ingested some sort of opium based drug and he is overdosing. The most appropriate treatment would include suction, applying high flow 02 via NRB, and administration of Narcan if protocols and scope of practice allow
b. He is hypoglycemic and has diabetes mellitus. The most appropriate treatment would include checking his blood sugar

level, putting him on high flow O2 via NRB, and administering glucose if necessary

c. He is hyperglycemic and extremely dehydrated. The most appropriate treatment would include administering high flow O2 via NRB, rapid transport, and a fluid bolus if scope of practice allows

d. He has been stuck in the neck by a poison dart. The most appropriate treatment would involve transporting him in a prone position to the hospital where an

Question 248: Your patient is an 8 year old girl who fell from a swing and hit her head. She has a pulse but is not breathing. Your CPR should include what?

a. Breaths at a rate of 12-20
b. Breaths at a rate of 10-12
c. Breaths at a rate of 20-30
d. Chest compressions and ventilations at a ratio of 30:2

Question 249: A report of a woman with an acute abdominal complaint comes in on the ambulance radio. You and your partner Lebomowitz arrive to find a 45-year-old woman holding her stomach. You perform a primary survey and administer oxygen via NRB as Lebomowitz begins history taking. According to the NREMT medical assessment skill sheet, what should you do next?

a. Get a set of baseline vitals
b. Assess breathing, pulse, and skin condition, then do a secondary survey
c. Do a detailed physical examination and then repeat the initial assessment
d. Do a secondary assessment focusing on her chief complaint

Question 250: A 26 year old woman has called the ambulance because she has begun delivery of her baby. Dispatch says the mother stated the baby's foot was sticking out of the vaginal opening. You should be prepared to?

a. High flow 02 on the mother, rapid transport, and gently maneuver the baby's foot back into the vagina
b. Place patient into a knee to chest position and rapid transport
c. Ask the mother to push and assist with the rest of the delivery
d. Gently pull the rest of the baby out by the foot sticking out

Answers

Question 1: You are dispatched to an amusement park where a 16-month-old boy is reported to have something wedged in his throat. Dispatch says that the child is breathing, but it sounds very noisy like a whistle. Upon arrival you can see that the child is breathing with stridor, is pale, and is beginning to turn blue around the lips. What is the best treatment plan for this patient?

c. Begin transport while giving blow-by oxygen. Continue to monitor the status of the child's airway en route to the hospital.

Rationale: The best choice is to begin transport while giving blow-by oxygen. As the child's airway is not completely occluded and he is still exchanging air, you should begin moving toward definitive care while providing additional oxygen. Using a mask to provide oxygen to a patient with a foreign body airway obstruction is contraindicated.

Question 2: You arrive on scene with your partner Stuart to a multi-car collision involving at least 6 patients. You have called for additional units to help you out with the scene. What should you do next?

c. Prioritize and triage the patients

Rationale: With more patients than you can manage, you need to prioritize and triage based on who has the worst injuries.

Question 3: You and your partner Bob are called to the scene of a man down. The report said the man has no pulse and that family members are doing CPR. Upon arriving at the scene what 3 things are you going to do first?

d. Attach the AED, tell everyone to stand back, and hit the analyze button

Rationale: Your gloves should be on prior to coming in contact with the patient. You would attach an AED and shock if indicated, according to AHA Guidelines.

Question 4: Dispatch has reported that there is a man passed out behind a supermarket and he is not breathing. You arrive to find a male sitting alone up against a wall. His eyes are closed and he does not respond to your attempts to elicit an answer. He is breathing at 8 irregular breaths per minute with periods of apnea. There is a baggy with a white substance on the ground next to him. When you give him a sternal rub, he grabs his chest with his hand, but does not make any noise. What is this man's GCS and what is the best course of action?

a. GCS of 7 / Assist ventilation via BVM

Rationale: This man needs assistance breathing. With the low rate and periods of apnea he is not getting enough oxygen. He does not open his eyes to any stimulus, so that is 1 point. He will not answer any questions or talk, so that is also 1 point. Finally he localizes pain by grabbing his chest, that would give you 5, for a total of 7.

Question 5: You are called to the scene of a man down. Dispatch reports the man is pulseless and bystanders are doing CPR. According to the NREMT Cardiac Arrest Management/AED skill sheet, which of the following sequences is appropriate?

d. Complete one cycle of CPR, Attach the AED, Have everyone stand clear during rhythm check

Rationale: Your gloves should be on! According to the NREMT skill sheet one cycle of CPR should be performed prior to attaching AED. Inserting an adjunct is not listed on this NREMT Skill Sheet.

Question 6: You arrive on scene for a possible poisoning. The patient is a 9 month old girl who was found with an open bottle of drain cleaner. She has a bump on her forehead and is noticeably irritable. During your assessment you note that the child does not make eye contact with you at all. Which of the following is the best course of action and why?

a. Initiate transport with blow by oxygen. The lack of eye contact and irritability are concerning signs in children this age.

Rationale: A child who is not making eye contact and acting irritable with a possible head or ingestion emergency should be transported immediately and given oxygen. Blow-by is an appropriate oxygen treatment for children.

Question 7: Your patient is a 33 year old female who fell off the back of a motorcycle going approximately 20 MPH. Her respirations are irregular at 8 a minute. An OPA has been inserted and ventilations are being assisted with a BVM and 100% O2 at a rate and tidal volume of_____. C-Spine precautions have been taken and she is packaged and moved to the ambulance where she stops breathing and there is no palpable pulse. CPR is started and the lead paramedic does a rapid sequence intubation. The BVM is attached to the ET tube and ventilations are restarted at a rate of _____.

a. 10 to 12 breaths per minute. Tidal volume of just enough air to give adequate chest rise. / 8 to 10 breaths per minute without pauses in compressions.

Rationale: With an OPA in, this woman should be receiving assisted ventilations at a rate of 10-12 breaths per minute, according to the newest AHA Guidelines, with a tidal volume of just enough air to give adequate chest rise. Milliliters of volume were found to be difficult if not impossible to estimate while delivering rescue breaths. Once the CPR starts with the advanced airway in place, the rate changes to 8 to 10 breaths per minute WITHOUT pauses in compressions.

Question 8: Your patient is a 58 year old female. She called 911 complaining of difficulty breathing. During your initial assessment, you find that she is using accessory muscles to breath at a rate of 20 shallow breaths per minute, and her SpO2 is 98% on room air. She has high pitched inspiratory stridor and is slightly cyanotic around her mouth. When you kneel down beside her you notice an ash tray piled high with cigarette butts. Which of the following is the most likely cause of her breathing difficulty, and what would be the most appropriate treatment?

d. She has a foreign body obstruction in her upper airway. You should encourage her to cough in an attempt to dislodge it. Give high flow O2 and rapid transport

Rationale: Inspiratory stridor is associated with an obstruction of the upper airway. This can be due to swelling, trauma, or an object that is lodged in place, allowing only partial air flow. Stridor on exhalation is associated with lower airway obstructions.

Question 9: Which of the following would not be considered an early sign of respiratory depression in a 7 year old girl?

d. Cyanosis of the lips

Rationale: All of the answer choices are EARLY signs of breathing problems in a child with the exception of Cyanosis. Cyanosis is a LATE sign.

Question 10: What is Post Traumatic Stress Disorder (PTSD)?

a. Stress encountered after an incident

Rationale: Stress encountered after an incident is called PTSD and can be a very serious obstacle for an EMS provider to deal with. It is important to communicate with other EMS providers and seek assistance if you are having trouble dealing with the stress from an incident. Most often incidents involving pediatrics or other care providers are the most difficult to process. Never be afraid to ask for help.

Question 11: Which of the following choices is not a route of drug administration?

a. Nuchal

Rationale: Nuchal is not a route of medication administration, It is a term to describe a critical situation sometimes found during childbirth.

Question 12: You and your partner Stacy are called to an apartment complex for a 17 year old female complaining of abdominal pain. Upon entering the residence you see the patient looking pale and lying on the couch. Her abdomen is completely distended and she has a towel in her lap with traces of blood on it. Her respirations are at 20 breaths per minute and her pulse is 114. She denies any trauma and tells you she has a small amount of vaginal bleeding. After applying high flow O2 and moving her to the ambulance, you discover a loop of tissue protruding from the patients vagina. What is likely happening with this patient and how would you treat her?

d. She has a prolapsed cord. Insert a gloved hand into the vagina and check for pulsations in the cord. Gently lift child's head off of the cord and transport in a supine position with the hips elevated. Treat for shock and establish IV en route if scope of practice allows.

Rationale: This patient is most likely delivering a child and has a prolapsed cord. A loop of umbilical cord emerges from the vagina first prior to any part of the baby. The danger is that the cord can become compressed between the baby's head and the mothers pelvis interfering with blood flow to the baby. If the cord is pulsing, it is a good sign. Do not, at anytime, push the protruding part back into the vagina. Use a warm and moist sterile towel to cover the umbilical cord.

Question 13: You arrive on scene with your partner Elija to a multiple vehicle accident where you are the 2nd ambulance to arrive. Scene size up indicates there are 7 patients in 3 cars all requiring extrication. In the first car is a 27 year old woman who is 32 weeks pregnant, conscious, and crying, a 12 year old girl who is screaming and complaining of back pain, and an 8 year old boy who has a facial laceration and open fracture of the tibia who is also conscious but breathing very shallow. In the second car is an 86 year old man who is slumped against the steering wheel with no pulse and has a piece of metal impaled through his head. In the third car are 3 teenagers 17 years of age. The two in the front seat are complaining of neck pain and appear to have an altered level of consciousness. Neither of them were wearing a seatbelt and both have contusions on their foreheads. In the back seat is the last occupant, a girl who said she was having a seizure and vomiting earlier so her friends were taking her to the hospital. She was wearing her seat belt and has no sign of injury. Who should be receiving treatment first?

b. The 8 year old boy

Rationale: The 86 year old man shows signs that resuscitation would be futile. The eight year old boy has similar injuries to the other patients, but is the only one having breathing difficulties.

Question 14: A call comes in for a 61 yr old female with an altered LOC. When you arrive, the patient's sister tells you that the patient had a stroke about a year ago, but she knows of no other health problems. During your initial assessment, you find her eyes open and looking around. She is speaking to you, but saying inappropriate words. She will not obey your commands to "raise your arm please ma'am" and she moves her arm toward her chest when you give her a light sternal rub. What is this woman's GCS and what should you do after administering oxygen?

a. GCS of 12 / Package the patient for transport

Rationale: The woman's eyes are open spontaneously so she gets a 4. She is speaking inappropriate words and this gets her a 3. You know she will not obey commands, but will localize pain which gets her a 5, which nets her a GCS of 12. Given the history and the altered LOC, immediate transport is the next best thing to do.

Question 15: Fluid that accumulates in the lungs makes the transfer of oxygen more difficult as the alveoli are partitioned by the fluid. This condition is called?

c. Pulmonary edema

Rationale: Edema is the build up of fluids. In the case of the lungs it prevents efficient oxygen exchange.

Question 16: Dispatch has just called you to Frontier Lake where a man's boat has capsized. The update is the patient is likely suffering from hypothermia and is breathing very shallow. You and your partner Sean arrive to find a man and a woman doing CPR on an approximately 48 year old male. When you and Sean begin CPR, what rate and depth of compressions will you use?

a. 30:2 / at least 2 inches

Rationale: AHA guidelines specify that for adult CPR a 30:2 ratio of compressions to breaths is to be used. Additionally, the depth of compressions should be at least 2 inches for adults. This question is also used to demonstrate that often times, the call you receive from dispatch is not the call at which you arrive. Be prepared for anything.

Question 17: You are the triage officer at a multiple casualty incident, and you are applying tags to each of the 5 patients. Patient 1 has a fractured tibia and is complaining of back pain. Patient 2 has a GCS of 6 with snoring respirations. Patient 3 has a broken finger. Patient 4 has no pulse and no respirations. Patient 5 has severe burns and a broken left radius. Which of the following choices provides the correct tag to patient combination?

b. 1Yellow, 2Red, 3Green, 4Black, 5Red

Rationale: The first patient is yellow, with a broken arm and back pain, their transport can be delayed. The second patient has a diminished LOC and is having problems breathing, so they are a priority one or red tag. The third patient only has a broken finger, which is minor, so they are a green tag and will be transported last. Patient 4, without a pulse and respirations, is a black tag with little hope of recovery. Patient number 5 is a red tag with severe burns.

Question 18: Your patient has a distended abdomen which you know can disrupt proper movement of the diaphragm and lead to?

d. Hypoventilation

Rationale: If the diaphragm cannot move very well it inhibits breathing and poor breathing will lead to low oxygen levels or hypoxia.

Question 19: How many compressions per minute would you give an adult patient who has no pulse?

b. 100-120 compressions per minute

Rationale: 2010 AHA guidelines now require at least 100 compressions per minute, however you can do more. The best option is 100-120 compressions per minute.

Question 20: You and your partner Zoe arrive on scene to find an 8 year old girl who was struck by an ice cream truck while crossing the street. She is unresponsive and has an abrasion on her forehead and an abrasion on her right side. She is breathing at 20 breaths per minute with adequate depth. What would be the most appropriate action to take at this point?

a. Take C-spine precautions and Administer O2 via nasal canula at 6 LPM

Rationale: Her respirations are within range and she was just struck by a car. C-spine precautions and oxygen would be the best choice of those given.

Question 21: An Incident Command System is designed to:

d. Manage and control emergency responders and resources

Rationale: Incident Command Systems are utilized to manage resources and responders and are very useful in mass casualty events and scenes that contain hazardous materials.

Question 22: You are about to begin CPR on a patient .You go to open their airway when you realize that CPR will probably not be advised. Which of the following answers could be a reason not to administer CPR?

d. The patient has a stiff neck and jaw

Rationale: A stiff neck and jaw may be a sign of rigor mortis and CPR would prove futile.

Question 23: Your patient doesn't remember what happened. She is sweating, incontinent, and has a bleeding tongue. What do you suspect happened to this patient?

d. The patient experienced a seizure

Rationale: The most likely cause of these symptoms is a seizure. While there is a possibility of a head injury, you don't normally find the sweating and tongue bites with this scenario. A patient who is hypoglycemic or who overdoses on medications doesn't normally have tongue bites either.

Question 24: You and your partner Aaron arrive on scene to find a 10 year old boy who was struck by a car while chasing a cat into the street. He is unresponsive to painful stimuli and has a large abrasion on his right side. He is breathing at 24 respirations per minute and regular. Your next course of action would be...?

d. Put a C collar on him

Rationale: His respirations are within range and he was just struck by a car. C spine precautions would be what you should do next.

Question 25: You are the lone EMT stationed at a local sporting event when you witness a man collapse from an apparent cardiac arrest. You have all of the equipment that you would need for a cardiac arrest event with you. Your best course of action would be?

b. Attach the AED, hook it up, and analyze

Rationale: AHA CPR Guidelines say that when an adult cardiac arrest is witnessed and an AED is immediately available on site, defibrillation should be the first priority. If there were no AED immediately available and there were two EMTs it would be best for one EMT to perform CPR while the other retrieves the AED.

Question 26: What is the first stage of labor?

c. The cervix is dilating

Rationale: The cervix dilates and thins during the 1st stage of labor. During the 2nd stage the baby enters the birth canal. From delivery of the infant on to delivering of the placenta is the 3rd stage.

Question 27: Approximately how many ambulance crashes happen each year in the United States?

c. 6,000

Rationale: Approximately 6000 ambulance crashes a year. According to the Center for Disease Control and Prevention there were 300 fatal ambulance crashes with 275 pedestrians and motorists killed between 1991 and 2001. Of the passengers on board the ambulances 82 patients were killed and 27 EMS providers. This data does not include the thousands of others injured.

Question 28: You are transporting a 27-year-old female who was the driver in a single car MVA on a remote logging road. She is on oxygen at 12LPM and had an actively bleeding laceration on her scalp that has been controlled with pressure. Her pulse is 100 with respirations of 12 a minute and her blood pressure is 110/70. You are still 30 to 40 minutes from the hospital. According to the NREMT trauma management skill sheet, which of the following answer choices contains the best treatment for this patient given the circumstances.

d. Reassess and treat any conditions that present

Rationale: The patient has been treated, packaged, and baseline vital signs have been taken. The final step on the NREMT Trauma Assessment Skill sheet would be the reassessment and ongoing treatment of the patient.

Question 29: You arrive on scene with your partner Steve to a 1-vehicle accident. You are the 1st ambulance to arrive. Scene size up indicates there are 4 patients in the car. In the front is a 45 year old woman who is unconscious and wearing her seat belt, a 7 year old girl who is unrestrained and complaining of finger pain, an 8 year old boy who is unrestrained and has no signs or symptoms, and a 5 year old girl who is unrestrained and has no signs or symptoms. There is little to no damage to the car and it appears as if she just went off the road at a very slow rate of speed and bumped up against a fence. What could have likely been the cause of the woman's altered LOC?

a. Diabetic reaction, alcohol, stroke, or seizure

Rationale: Diabetes, alcohol, stroke, or seizure are all likely in this situation as no one in the car is injured. Her altered LOC could have been caused by any of the things listed above (they are more likely than any of the other answers).

Question 30: Your 57 year old patient was a chain smoker for 35 years and is pursing his lips during exhalation. How does this action assist the patients respiratory effort?

a. It creates a backpressure on collapsed alveoli

Rationale: Breathing with pursed lips is a sign that a chronic obstructive pulmonary disease (COPD) patient is trying to keep the alveoli open with backpressure on their lungs.

Question 31: An ice storm has caused a 10 car pile up on a nearby interstate. Incident command has instructed you to take over triage of the patients. Patient 1 is a woman who has a broken arm and a back injury with suspected spinal cord damage. Patient 2 is male and has a broken femur and is showing signs of shock. Patient 3 is an elderly woman who has a laceration on her forehead and pain in her wrist. Patient 4 is a male, breathing at 6 breaths a minute with a head injury. What color triage tag should each of these patients receive?

d. 1Yellow, 2Red, 3Green, 4Red

Rationale: The first patient with the back injury is yellow tagged, even with the suspected spinal cord injury, their transport is delayed. Patient number 2 is a red tagged because of the signs of shock, they require immediate transport. Patient number 3 has only minor injuries, therefore, she gets a green tag and is transported last. Patient number 4 is having problems breathing, so it is priority one or red tag.

Question 32: You and your partner are at lunch when you are called to a scene of a 3 yr old who does not have a pulse and is not breathing. You and your partner discuss what depth of compression should be given and you agree that it is?

c. At least 1/3rd the depth of the chest

Rationale: According to 2010 AHA guidelines at least 1/3rd of the depth of the anterior posterior diameter of the chest should be compressed when performing CPR on a child.

Question 33: The body's first physiological response to a deep laceration is _____.

a. To stop it by chemical means and vasoconstriction (hemostasis)

Rationale: Localized constriction of the vessels, formation of a platelet plug, and coagulation are the initial steps the body takes to stop the bleeding.

Question 34: Dispatch reports a jet ski collision on a local lake. The reporting party says that the two guys are in the water floating face down and one of their buddies just jumped off the boat to help them. When you arrive on scene the boat has just brought the two unconscious men to shore and CPR and rescue breathing are in progress. The first man has a pulse but is not breathing. The second man does not have a pulse and is apneic. What ventilation rate will you use for the first man? What about the second man?

d. 10-12 ventilations per minute for the first man and 6 ventilations per minute and 100 compressions for the second man

Rationale: The AHA guidelines specify that an adult who is apneic, but has a pulse, should have rescue breathing performed on them at a rate of 10-12 ventilations per minute. (mouth to mask or BVM ventilations). An adult who is pulseless and apneic should have CPR performed on him/her at a rate of 30 compressions to 2 ventilations. This ratio creates a ventilation rate of approximately 6 ventilations per minute with at least 100 compressions.

Question 35: You respond to a call of a house fire where the first unit on scene has reported burn injuries to a child that are classified as "minor". Minor burns for a child would be?

d. Partial thickness burns on one arm

Rationale: Unless it is a hand, foot, face, or genitals, anything less than 10% and partial thickness is considered minor. The full circumference of one arm accounts for 9% BSA, but would be considered critical due to the potential for compartment syndrome.

Question 36: You arrive on scene of a shooting where law enforcement has secured the scene. Which of the following answers contain the most accurate sequence of actions according to the NREMT trauma management skill sheet?

a. Determine the number of patients - Consider C-spine stabilization - Assess the patient's airway - Get a set of vital signs

Rationale: The only answer in the correct sequence is the first. All others have 2 steps out of order OR are not even on the trauma skill sheet. Be sure to practice these sheets DIRECTLY from the NREMT as variations and or outdated versions are often printed in text books. The NREMT has recently updated many of their skills sheets so make sure you have the most current version directly from https://www.nremt.org/nremt/about/exam_coord_man.asp

Question 37: What life-threatening disease is caused by abnormally low levels of corticosteroid hormones produced by the adrenal glands which causes weight loss, weakness, hypotension, and gastrointestinal disorders?

b. Addison Disease

Rationale: Addison disease is a shrinking of the adrenal tissue and not being able to produce enough corticosteroid hormones to meet the requirements of the body, it is a rare and life-threatning disease. Cushing syndrome is the opposite of Addisons disease where the adrenal glands produce too much corticosteroid hormones. Thyrotoxicosis is overproduction of the thyroid gland and is commonly known as hyperthyroidism. Thyroid Storm is a life threatening condition from overactivity of the thyroid gland.

Question 38: You are responding the the scene of a possible drowning. Dispatch resports that a 3 year old girl was found face down in the family swimming pool. In this case the use of lights and sirens would be:

d. Used as a device to ask other drivers for the right-of-way

Rationale: According to NEMS ES EMR audible warning devices are to be used for asking others for the right of way and are NOT to be used for clearing traffic

Question 39: A 6 year old child has fallen from the monkey bars at the local park. What are the components of the pediatric assessment triangle (PAT) that you would use to rapidly assess this patient?

b. Appearance, Work of breathing, Circulation

Rationale: The pediatric assessment triangle (PAT) is utilized to rapidly assess and form a general impression of the child's condition. Their Appearance (mental status and muscle tone,',',',',2), Work of breathing or visually determining their respiratory status, and assessing Circulation of their skin, will give you a good idea of their distress level.

Question 40: A respiration rate would be considered within normal limits for an adult at____ per minute, for a 6-12 year old child at ____ per minute, and for an infant at____ per minute.

b. 16 - 25 - 40

Rationale: According to the NES, normal adult respiratory rates are from 16-20, school age children (6-12) are 20-30, and infants are initially 40-60 and then drop to 30-40 after the first few minutes. Note: Respiratory rates for late adulthood, 61+, is dependent on the patient's physical and health status.

Question 41: You have just assisted in the delivery of a baby boy. The child is pink, but his arms and legs are blue. His pulse rate is 90 beats per minute. He is not making any sound and is showing limited movement. His respirations are slow and irregular. What is this newborn's APGAR score and how should he be treated?

b. 4 / Stimulate the newborn by rubbing his spine. Use clean towels to dry him off and place him at the level of the mother's vagina.

Rationale: APGAR is Appearance, Pulse, Grimace, Activity, and Respirations. If the child's core is pink, but the appendages are blue, it is worth 1 point. A pulse below 100 beats per minute is awarded 1 point. No grimace/cough or sneeze is given 0 points. Limited movement or activity is awarded 1 point and slow irregular breathing is awarded 1 point for a total APGAR score of 4. Don't swat the baby while hanging upside down as this is an unacceptable and unnecessary method of stimulation.

Question 42: Which type of diabetic emergency generally has a rapid onset?

c. Hypoglycemia

Rationale: Diabetic coma comes on over a period of hours or days. Hypoglycemic or insulin shock happens in minutes to hours.

Question 43: You have requested helicopter transportation of a critical burn patient. The remote nature of the accident will force the helicopter to land on an incline. From which direction should you approach the helicopter?

d. The downhill side

Rationale: Approaching from the downhill side of the helicopter is the safest route in this situation.

Question 44: Someone who is U on the AVPU scale would require what type of secondary assessment?

a. Rapid full-body scan

Rationale: Unconscious patients require a rapid full-body scan to rule out trauma. If a patient is able to communicate, you can focus on the areas they indicate are injured.

Question 45: A fierce winter storm has left hundreds of people stranded along a stretch of highway for a few days. You have been dispatched with the National Guard to help care for anyone suffering from exposure. As you prepare your equipment what things should you carry extra of and why?

b. Drinking water; Dehydration is a very likely problem

Rationale: While warming methods and glucose are good, drinking water is probably the most important. This is due to the fact that cold weather decreases our thirst mechanism and so we don't drink. However, a lot of moisture is lost during the respiratory cycle in cold air. This is compounded by not feeling thirsty, and a person becomes dehydrated very quickly and doesn't realize it. It is important to encouraging patients of exposure to take fluids either hot or cold.

Question 46: You are preparing to suction secretions from your patient's airway, when would you engage the suction action in the catheter?

b. While suctioning secretions and withdrawing the catheter

Rationale: You should only apply suction once you have the tip in the visible secretions and then continue suctioning on the way out. You should make a good effort to remove all secretions and try to limit your suctioning time to 10 or 15 seconds. If your patient's airway is completely full of secretions it may take a little longer. Remember that you need to clear the airway before ventilation begins to prevent aspiration, but also any suctioning you are doing is removing air from the patients airway as well.

Question 47: Unoxygenated blood travels into the lungs via the?

b. Pulmonary artery

Rationale: Blood travels into the lungs from the pulmonary artery. This is the only artery in the body that carries unoxygenated blood.

Question 48: Which of the following is NOT considered a common side effect of nitroglycerin?

a. Bradypnea

Rationale: Nitro is likely to cause headaches and changes in pulse rate but not normally associated with slowing the breathing down to abnormal rates.

Question 49: Who is responsible for developing protocols for an EMS system?

b. Medical director

Rationale: The medical director is responsible for creating these written instructions for various medical conditions and injuries.

Question 50: Name three medical conditions that often cause tachypnea?

a. Hypoxia, CHF, shock

Rationale: Hypoxia, congestive heart failure (CHF), and shock are correct for the following reasons. Hypoxia is a condition in which the body or region of the body is starved of oxygen supply which in turn causes the body to become acidodic. Tachypnea is often the result because it increases alveolar PO2 by raising the rate and depth of breathing. Congestive heart failure is where the ventricular myocardium becomes so damaged that it can no longer keep up with the return flow of blood from the atria. The lungs become congested with fluid once the heart fails to pump blood effectively. Blood then backs up in the pulmonary veins which leads to a decrease in oxygen exchange at the capillary level (Pulmonary Edema). The body tries to compensate by becoming tachypnic. Shock: Cardiovascular system fails to provide sufficient circulation for every body part to perform its function. Due to the poor perfusion, metabolic acidosis occurs early in the process. The body will then become tachypnic while trying to compensate for the metabolic acidosis and establish homeostasis.

Question 51: You arrive at an apartment building where a man has been reported unconscious. You enter the room to find him lying supine in his bed with his wife at his side. Respirations are rapid and shallow at 24 breaths per minute and you are unable to get a response from him. His wife says he is a diabetic and that she just lanced his finger to measure his glucose when you arrived. What would be the best course of action?

d. Administer high flow O2 Assess circulation - Make a transport decision

Rationale: The only answer that has a correct order of treatment is administer O2, check circulation, and make a transport decision. This is according to the NREMT medical assessment skill sheet. On the other answers: You would not start this treatment with glucose. You would not perform an intervention without getting some baselines. Ventilating a patient at 10-12 who is breathing at 24 is near impossible.

Question 52: Dispatch has called you and your partner Libby to an ATV accident in the foothills of a nearby mountain range. You come on scene to find a 60 yr old man lying in a weeded area off to the side of the road. He apparently lost control of the four wheeler and it rolled several times. According to the NREMT spinal immobilization skill sheet, which of the following answer choices contain your MOST accurate sequence of steps?

b. Direct assistant to maintain manual immobilization of the head - Check circulation and motor sensory - Apply C -collar

Rationale: According to the NREMT spinal immobilization skill sheet answer number 2 is in the best sequence. The first answer does not check CMS before intervention and that would be failure. The third and fourth answer do not utilize a c-collar/backboard for immobilization prior to moving the patient.

Question 53: You are called to the scene of a woman who is having difficulty breathing. Upon arrival you notice several people surrounding the woman who seems to be agitated. Your scene assessment determines it to be safe and you approach the woman who is in the tripod position. Her breathing is rapid and shallow. She states her ribs hurt after being struck with a punch from her husband. You should?

b. Treat the patient if the situation appears safe and inform law enforcement of the possible assault when the time is appropriate

Rationale: If you believe the scene to be safe and begin treating the patient, it would be prudent to inform the police of the supposed attack.

Question 54: You are assessing the vital signs of a 7-year-old child. Which of the following sets of vitals would you hope to find?

c. BP 108/64, respirations of 20 per minute and a pulse of 100

Rationale: The only one of the answers that has all vitals falling within normal range is the 3rd choice. Each of the other choices has either one or two vitals out of normal range.

Question 55: You and your partner Warren arrive at a house where a woman in her 50's has been reported unconscious. Her pulse is 80 and she is apneic. Warren inserts an oropharyngeal and you begin ventilating her at _____. After about 1 minute of ventilations, the patient begins to have seizures and is gagging. What would be the most appropriate thing to do?

c. 10-12 breaths per minute/ Remove the oropharyngeal

Rationale: The AHA says that with a simple oral adjunct, this patient should get 10-12 ventilations per minute. If the patient has a gag reflex, you must remove the OPA. There is a good possibility they may vomit as well, so having suction ready is a good idea.

Question 56: You arrive on scene to find a female patient actively having contractions every 10-12 minutes apart. A visual inspection of the patient reveals no visible crowning. Which stage of labor would you consider this patient to be in?

a. 1st stage of labor.

Rationale: The first stage of labor is dilation of the cervix. This can have contractions at varying intervals, and can also have some blood spotting or the breaking of the 'waters'. It ends when the cervix is fully dilated. The second stage of labor begins at that point and continues until the baby has been fully delivered. The third stage is the delivery of the umbilicus and placenta. The fourth stage is usually referred to as the period of time after delivery of the placenta and is not referenced in all textbooks. In the pre-hospital setting it is difficult to know if your patient is still in the first or second stage of labor since we don't check for cervical dilation. One good way to know is to understand that the urge to push comes after the cervix is dilated, so this is a great indicator that the patient has moved beyond stage 1 and is now in stage 2.

Question 57: You are dispatched on a medical call to a 45 year old male who is exhibiting signs of a stroke. His wife told dispatch that her husband's speech is slurred and he appears to be having seizures. When you arrive on scene, the man is sweating profusely in a postictal state and breathing at 16 breaths a minute with adequate volume and regularity. What elements of the assessment would likely be the most useful right now?

b. History and blood glucose measurement

Rationale: This patient, while exhibiting signs of stroke, is also exhibiting signs of hypoglycemia. Requesting some history from the wife may uncover that the man is a diabetic. A glucose measurement can confirm or disprove the hypoglycemia and allow you to further your differential diagnoses. The other answers each contain assessment elements and tools that would also be utilized, but none would be more useful than answer 2.

Question 58: You are called to a neighborhood pool where a 5 year old girl was found floating unconscious. She is cyanotic and has no muscle tone. Your partner Greg does not find a pulse and the child is not breathing. Your CPR should include a compression to ventilation ratio of_____ and each compression should be at a depth of_____.

b. 15:2 / one third the diameter of the chest

Rationale: AHA CPR Guidelines specify that 2 person infant/child CPR by health care professionals should be done at a 15:2 ratio. Each chest compression should be 1/3 the anterior-posterior diameter of the chest.

Question 59: You have been called to a bowling alley for an unknown medical. A 50ish male is lying supine in the parking lot and there is a crowd of people around him. There is no sign of trauma. He is breathing deep, regular, and rapid with his arms crossed over his chest. There is a small puddle of orange colored vomit next to his head. He will not respond to you and his pants are saturated with what appears to be urine. There is a full bottle of whiskey laying next to him on the cement. What is most likely wrong with this man, and what would be the best choice of treatment?

c. He is a diabetic who ran out of insulin and now he is hyperglycemic. A fluid bolis and oxygen via NRB

Rationale: He is not likely hypoglycemic as all of the signs point to hyperglycemia and are not indicative of hypoglycemia. It is possible that he was hit by a car, but the signs, including the unbroken bottle of whiskey on the cement, make it unlikely and inappropriate to jump to such a conclusion. While he could have also had a drug overdose, the signs point elsewhere. The treatment of inserting an OPA is not necessary as his airway appears patent.

Question 60: Which of the following would you expect to find in an infant who is breathing adequately?

b. Belly breathing

Rationale: Belly breathing is normal for infants and young children. Accessory muscle use, retractions of the intercostals, and respirations of 15 breaths per minute, are signs that the child is not breathing adequately.

Question 61: NIMS is best explained as:

d. A template system for providing consistent, effective processes in preparing for, responding to, and recovering from an incident

Rationale: The National Incident Management System is designed as a template system for providing consistent, effective processes in preparing for, responding to, and recovering from an incident.

Question 62: You and your partner Asher arrive on scene to find a woman who has had a syncopal episode at her daughter's wedding. It was brought on, she says, by witnessing for the first time a dragon tattoo on the ankle of her daughter as she walked down the isle. Guests at the wedding state that she was eased to the ground and did not fall and hit anything. After laying supine for 10 minutes she was helped to her feet with no complaints. She is pale, but has all function and has a GCS of 15. This woman likely suffered what?

a. Psychogenic shock

Rationale: Once a person suffering from psychogenic shock has been allowed to stay supine for a few minutes, they generally improve perfusion and circulatory function again.

Question 63: It's 20 degrees outside and your unit has been called to an apartment complex where a man is having trouble breathing. You arrive to find the man sitting in a tripod position on a bench. He has a portable O2 tank and is receiving oxygen via a nasal cannula at 3 LPM. Your initial assessment reveals that his breathing is rapid with minimal chest rise and fall. Respiration rate is 20 breaths per minute and his pulse is 130. In a hoarse voice the man tells you he has a history of COPD and is on a new medication which he is unable to name. He denies any chest pain, but says he is getting a headache. Which of the following scenarios is most likely the cause for this man's breathing difficulties and how would you treat him?

a. He is having an allergic reaction to the new COPD medication. Move him to the ambulance and administer high flow 02 via NRB

Rationale: Given the signs and symptoms, breathing difficulty, hoarse voice, tachycardia, increased respiration rate, new medication, and headache the most likely scenario is the allergic reaction to the new medication. Answer 2 is incorrect because COPD drugs are not designed to remove surfactant from the alveoli. Also, you would not give him high flow O2 via a cannula. Answer 3 is not likely correct as live bees are not found in 20 degree temperatures. Additionally, taking a blood pressure prior to administration of the Epi pen is recommended unless you are certain there is life threatening airway compromise due to an acute allergic reaction.

Question 64: Why does the NHTSA require use of lights and sirens during response and transportation?

b. The NHTSA does NOT require use of lights and sirens during response and transportation

Rationale: Lights and sirens can be used at the responder's discretion to move through traffic more efficiently in order to speed up transport in a safe manner. They can be used for alerting people to your presence, but may also cause anxiety in patients as well as drivers around you, causing them to do stu.... unintelligent things (the drivers not the patients!). The NHTSA does NOT require the use of lights and sirens during response and transport. Each EMS call has a priority and local systems may opt to run 'non-code' for many types of calls and transports.

Question 65: You and your partner Genovese suspect a significant MOI to a patient who has been in a high-speed front end collision. In what order should you do your assessment?

a. Primary survey - SAMPLE history - Secondary assessment

Rationale: According to the newest NREMT trauma assessment skill sheet, a primary survey should be followed by history taking and then a secondary assessment.

Question 66: You respond to a call of a man down in a very rough neighborhood. Upon entering the location of the call you notice a group of young men in a fist fight at what appears to be the address of the call. There are two men on the ground not moving and your lights and sirens have frightened the other men away. What should you do next?

a. Call for police to secure the scene and wait for them to arrive

Rationale: As much as you want to help the injured you must be sure the scene is safe first and you cannot do that without police help in this instance.

Question 67: You arrive on scene with your partner Zelda to a restaurant where a woman is apparently having a reaction to the seafood from the buffet. She is having trouble breathing and her lips are swollen. Zelda hands you an adult EPI pen and you inject the patient into the thigh and hold it there for about 10 seconds. How long will the injection likely be effective?

c. 10-20 minutes

Rationale: Plan for it lasting only 10-20 minutes. Having additional dosages on hand during transport is a necessity.

Question 68: Your local Emergency Medical System is regulated by:

d. Your state EMS office.

Rationale: All Emergency Medical Systems are regulated by the state EMS office.

Question 69: A woman has fallen 20 ft. from a ski lift. You are the first medical unit on scene. She is conscious and breathing normally. C spine is in place and you package her on a backboard with high flow O2 and begin transport. The patient is looking around the ambulance and begins using inappropriate words to describe things she is seeing. You have given her several requests to wiggle her toes but she does not respond. This woman has a GCS of what?

a. 8

Rationale: Using inappropriate words gets her 3 points, spontaneous eye movement gets her 4, and no motor response on request gets her 1 point, for a total of 8 points.

Question 70: Without any further information, what condition would you say the following patient is in? A 1-year-old male with a pulse rate of 110, breathing at 30 breaths per minute, with a systolic BP of 90.

a. Good

Rationale: All vitals are within normal limits for a child of this age. 1-year-old is the dividing line between infancy and toddler age, and so both sets of vital sign ranges could apply to a 1-year-old. Treat the patient based on overall appearance and what the parents tell you is normal or abnormal.

Question 71: Your patient was the restrained passenger in a vehicle accident. She is complaining of back pain and shortness of breath. The proper way to remove this patient from the car is?

a. Using a seated immobilization device and then moving her to a backboard

Rationale: Using a KED or similar device with a seated patient and then transferring them to a backboard is the proper method of packaging this patient, provided there is no scene safety issues. You should provide high-flow oxygen to this patient and monitor her airway as well.

Question 72: You are dispatched to a boat fire with multiple victims in the water. You are the only Paramedic on scene. Upon arrival you find patient #1 shivering uncontrollably, but able to answer questions appropriately. Patient #2 is on a boat across the bay with another EMS unit. That unit relates that the patient is mildly hypothermic and doesn't want to be transported. Both patients indicate that a third person was with them and that he was burned badly. On scene command confirms that this patient is still in the water. Which is the most critical patient, and why?

c. Patient #3, because he will require the most care when he is removed from the water.

Rationale: Patient #3 is triaged as the most critical, even though you haven't seen him. Patient #1 is in mild hypothermia, and can be treated at the BLS level with warming measures. Patient #2 has been assessed and is refusing transport, so he is not your concern. There is no such thing as hypogenic shock.

Question 73: You arrive on scene and find an elderly man who has a history of hypertension. He takes medication daily for it to be regulated. He is feeling dizzy, his pulse is 70 and his BP is 110/70. Which is the most likely cause of his symptoms?

a. He is in shock

Rationale: Patients taking high blood pressure medications can be in shock and maintain a regular looking pulse. Medications may be preventing pulse and blood pressure from rising in shock as well.

Question 74: You and your partner Domonica are called to the scene of a single car MVA with two patients. The reporting party told dispatch that one of the patients is unconscious in the car and the other is out of the car and conscious, but bleeding badly from his face. You arrive to find that the man in the car is actually dead and the other man is standing up against a bystander's car. According to the NREMT Patient Assessment/Management - Trauma Skill Sheet what would be the most appropriate treatment for this patient?

d. Consider stabilization of the spine, Perform a primary survey and make a transport decision, then do a secondary assessment

Rationale: If you do not consider c-spine stabilization when appropriate you fail one of the critical criteria of this skill station. If you do a secondary assessment before assessing the ABC's you fail a critical criteria for this station as well. There is no such thing as a detailed focused exam.

Question 75: You are dispatched to a daycare where a child is having difficulty breathing. The caregiver called 911 and reported that the 5-year-old went down for a nap. When she went to check on him 30 minutes later he did not appear to be breathing normally. En route to this call, what are the most important things to remember?

c. Because of the size of a child's head you may need additional padding under the shoulders to align the airway. Flexion and hyperextension can obstruct the airway.

Rationale: You are being called for breathing difficulty. The most important initial considerations should revolve around making sure the child's airway is open. Understanding the anatomical differences in a child is necessary to ensure that the intervention of physically opening the airway is done properly. Properly dealing with the airway issue is your primary concern. You can deal with any possible legal issues after taking care of the patient.

Question 76: Your unit is called to the scene of a motor vehicle collision at a busy intersection. A man in his 40's, driving a small truck, has hit a telephone pole head on. He was unrestrained and ejected through the windshield at approximately 50 MPH. When you arrive, he has been secured to a backboard with proper c-spine precautions. His pulse is 80 beats per minute and he is breathing regularly and deeply at 12 respirations per minute. You notice that his pulse seems to weaken during inhalation. While taking his blood pressure, you see that each time he inhales, his systolic pressure drops by 20-30 mmHg. His trachea is midline and lung sounds are equal. What is the most likely reason for these vital signs?

b. Liquid filling the pericardium increases pressure and inhibits the ventricles from filling properly, which in turn leads to low stroke volume and low pressure

Rationale: This patient is exhibiting signs of cardiac tamponade and pulsus paradoxus, making answer 2 correct. Answer 1 is incorrect because the pons regulates respiration, but is not associated with pulse. Answer 3 is eluding to a tension pneumothorax, but the assessment confirms a midline trachea and equal breath sounds. Answer 4 is incorrect as injury to the spine will not cause an interference or a variant or irregular breathing pattern that causes a drop in blood pressure upon inspiration

Question 77: You and your partner Ramone have arrived at the scene of a house fire where 3 victims were pulled a safe distance from the home and are being attended by first responders. Your initial impression is of two women and a child lying unconscious on the ground. None appears to have been burned and their clothing is intact. None of the patients is breathing, but the second woman and the child do have a palpable pulse. At what rate would each of these patients be ventilated?

b. Woman one would get 12 breaths over 2 minutes. Woman two would get 20 to 24 breaths over 2 minutes and the child would get 24 to 40 breaths over 2 minutes

Rationale: Woman 1 does not have a pulse so you are doing CPR. With a 30:2 compression to ventilation ratio you would be delivering approximately 6 breaths per minute. Woman 2 has a pulse so she would only be given rescue ventilations at a rate of 10 to 12 per minute. The 3rd patient, the child has a pulse and would require rescue breathing at a rate of 12 to 20 respirations per minute.

Question 78: A woman's obstetrical history can be displayed using P and G. How would you display a woman's history who has had 3 pregnancies and 2 live births?

d. G3P2

Rationale: G3P2 would denote Gravida or number of pregnancies and Para or number of live births.

Question 79: A 46-year-old woman was hiking in the woods near her home when she accidentally stepped into a hive of hornets and was stung multiple times. She contacted 911 via her cell phone and is going to rendezvous with you at her residence. When you arrive at the home you find her lying on the front lawn. After completing your scene size up, which would be the most appropriate treatment sequence according to the NREMT Patient Assessment/Management - Medical Skill Sheet?

c. Determine level of consciousness - Identify life threats - Assess airway - breathing - and circulation

Rationale: On the first answer, you do not know what is wrong with this woman so you cannot assist her with epi after just a general impression. On the second answer, Giving O2 sounds like a good idea, but you missed the first three steps of the primary survey AND got vitals BEFORE doing a SAMPLE. On the fourth answer the first 3 steps of the primary survey were missed, and doing a secondary assessment is incorrect. Additionally, the injection of epi would have been administered during the ABC's if she were in anaphylaxis.

Question 80: You and your partner Abraham arrive on scene to a one-car collision with a cow. Your patient was driving about 45 MPH around a corner when the cow leaped from the roadside in front of the car. After doing your initial scene size up, which of the following would you proceed to?

b. Get a general impression of the patient

Rationale: According to the NREMT assessment skill sheets after the scene size up you should move to the primary survey/assessment, which begins with the general impression of the patient.

Question 81: What would be an expected systolic BP in infants, toddlers, and preschool aged children?

d. 80 mm Hg

Rationale: Infant 70-90, toddler 70-100, and preschool 80-110.

Question 82: A 27 year old man and his 4 year old nephew have been pulled from a river after being submerged for approximately 12 minutes. Rescue breathing for the man should include breaths at what rate? Rescue breathing for the child should include breaths at what rate?

a. 1 breath every 5-6 seconds for the man / 1 breath every 3-5 seconds for the child

Rationale: AHA CPR Guidelines specify state that adults should get 10-12 breaths per minute (one breath every 5-6 seconds). Children should get between 12-20 breaths per minute (one breath every 3-5 seconds). Old guidelines said 20 bpm for all infants and children. The new wider range is to allow the rescuer to tailor rescue breathing to the needs of the patient.

Question 83: You and your partner Grimes are called to the scene of a stabbing. There are two patients reported. A woman with a stab wound to the URQ and a man with a stab wound to the LRQ. The woman with the wound in the URQ is having problems breathing, has a pulse of 103, respirations of 35, and they are shallow. The patient with the stab wound to the LRQ is complaining of severe abdominal pain and has a pulse of 48 and a respiration rate of 24. Which patient is most likely to have a low blood pressure? Why?

a. The man, because of the nature and location of the injury, he may be losing blood internally. His pulse is too slow as well

Rationale: The man with the pulse of 48 and a knife wound to the lower right quadrant suggests internal bleeding which would lower the blood pressure.

Question 84: What would a baby that had a cephalic presentation during birth be considered?

d. Optimal for delivery

Rationale: Head first presentation is considered optimal for delivery of a baby through the vaginal opening.

Question 85: A call has come in for a possible drowning. You and your partner respond to a public swimming pool a few blocks from the station. A 9 year old boy apparently slipped while running, hit his head on the edge of the pool, and fell in. He has no pulse and he is not breathing. What would be your best choice of action?

d. Take manual stabilization of the boy's head and neck while additional rescuers ventilate at about 13 breaths per minute and provide at least 100 compressions per minute.

Rationale: AHA Guidelines state that two person health care provider CPR performed on a child should be done at a 15:2 ratio. This means you will deliver about 13 breaths a minute instead of the 5-6 delivered for an adult. Additionally, if a c-spine injury is suspected, as in this case, manual c-spine stabilization is now advised as mechanical/cervical may interterfere with CPR. Answer 2 does not address the absence of pulse and artificial ventilations are being delivered too fast.

Question 86: Which of the following statements is correct regarding the operation of an emergency vehicle:

d. Emergency vehicles must always be operated with due regard for the safety of others

Rationale: Even with limited privileges the driver of an emergency vehicle may still be held liable in a collision. You should never pass a school bus that is stopped to load or unload children. Emergency vehicles operating with lights and sirens are requesting the right of way from pedestrians and other drivers. Each state has different laws with regard to right of way privileges. Drivers and pedestrians in all states are not required to give the right of way to emergency vehicles.

Question 87: What are the main differences between a child's airway and an adult's airway?

c. A child's airway is narrower at the Cricoid ring and the tongue is larger in proportion to the mouth

Rationale: The proportions of a child's airway are different and the tongue takes up more space. The Cricoid cartilage is also the narrowest part of a child's airway.

Question 88: You and your partner Larry are dispatched to the call of a man with sever stomach pain. When you arrive on scene you find him lying on the floor of the kitchen in the fetal position. There is vomit on his face and he says he is going to throw up again. He denies falling and says the only thing wrong is that his stomach is killing him. Assessing his abdomen you find it to be very tender to the touch and he moans when you palpate his stomach. He is also breathing very fast at 30 a minute. What other signs and symptoms might you find with this patient?

a. Tachycardia - hypotension - fever

Rationale: The patient is not likely to have crepitus, having no pain and denying that they fell. A person with broken ribs is unlikely to be breathing fast and deep and if a person has been vomiting copius amounts it is likely they would be in metabolic alkalosis rather than acidosis.

Question 89: You arrive on scene to find a man in his 20's lying in a pool of vomit. You can see that he is breathing at about 16 breaths per minute and the depth of respiration is adequate. He has a small laceration on his forehead. You try getting a response by calling "Hey man can you hear me?" but he does not answer. Your partner gives him a quick sternal rub and his eyes pop open along with a whimper under his breath and then they close again. You ask him to perform several motor functions but he does not comply. He does not answer any of your questions. This man has a GCS of what?

c. 4

Rationale: Opening the eyes for pain nets 2 points, no verbal response gets 1 point, and no motor response nets 1 point for a total of 4 points.

Question 90: The symptoms of a TIA usually last around _____.

a. 1 minute

Rationale: The AHA (which is the source we will go by for the NREMT exam) states that most TIA's last less than 5 minutes with an average being only about 1 minute.
The National Institute of Neurological Disorders and Stroke state that a TIA is a transient stroke that lasts only a few minutes, but symptoms can persist for up to 24 hours. This is used to establish when a TIA becomes a stroke, ie. wait 24 hours and see.

Question 91: You and your partner are called to a swimming pool for a 5 year old who does not have a pulse and is not breathing. You begin CPR including compressions at what depth?

c. At least 1/3 the diameter of the chest

Rationale: 2010 AHA guidelines stipulate that at least 1/3rd of the anterior posterior diameter of the chest should be compressed while performing CPR on a child.

Question 92: You have just arrived at the scene to find a 27-year-old female complaining of anxiety and breathing difficulties. Which of the following questions would be most appropriate to ask first?

a. What is your name?

Rationale: When performing patient assessment, the first thing after your scene size-up is to do the primary survey (also called primary assessment). The first step of the primary survey is to form a general impression, followed by level of consciousness, then Airway, Breathing, and Circulatory status, and finally identify life threats during that process. While all of those questions are proper to ask at some point during an assessment, the best choice is to ask the patient her name first. This is critical information because it allows you to know who you are interacting with and helps to determine a general impression of the patient, according to their proper or improper response, and then determine airway status. This sets the stage for the rest of your assessment. You should always introduce yourself and ask for your patient's name at the beginning of your assessment. The other questions come during the history taking part of your assessment.

Question 93: EMT B Maloney is moving from an ambulance service in one state to a new ambulance service in another state. His new unit will accept his state license as an EMT B. This is an example of?

b. Reciprocity

Rationale: Reciprocity is the exchange of licensure or privileges, in this case from state to state.

Question 94: You arrive on scene with your partner Joe to find an 7 year old boy unconscious after being dragged from the water. He is not breathing and has no pulse. CPR in this case should include_____.

b. 15:2 compression to ventilation ratio

Rationale: AHA CPR Guidelines specify that for two person CPR on a child you should use a 15:2 ratio. It would be 30:2 if you were alone and did not have your partner Joe.

Question 95: In order to manuever an ambulance efficiently around a turn the driver should know the proper speed, _____ as well as understand the need to

_____.

b. the current position and projected path / reach the apex late in the turn

Rationale: When making a turn it is best to reach the apex late in the turn as the vehicle will tend to stay on the inside and maintain the traffic lane. If the apex is reached early it has a tendance to push the vehicle to the outside of the lane as it exits the curve.

Question 96: You are transporting a 6 year old child that has had a seizure. She is in the postictal state. How would you best describe this patient?

c. The patient is unresponsive with deep and rapid respirations

Rationale: The state at the end of a seizure where the patient is no longer having active seizures is called postictal. During the postictal state the patient's muscles relax and the breathing becomes deep and rapid in an attempt to compensate for the buildup of acids in the body. The patient usually begins breathing normally after several minutes as the body pH goes back to normal. Most commonly the patient is lethargic, confused, or unresponsive. While not as common, a patient may exhibit one-sided weakness like a stroke. However, unlike a stroke, this usually resolves rather quickly. Patients can become combative as they begin to regain consciousness and their minds try to determine where they are and what has happened. Always be prepared for this possibility. If your patient doesn't improve and remains unresponsive or lethargic for a long time, you might want to consider some other possible underlying problems like hypoglycemia or a system infection of some kind.

Question 97: You arrive at a restaurant to a call of a woman choking. You find her sitting in a chair, very pale, and sweating. She states in a very hush tone that she has a piece of steak caught in her throat. You should immediately?

d. Encourage her to cough as it is likely high enough in the airway to expel it

Rationale: Unless her airway is completely blocked you should not attempt Heimlich thrusts. If she can speak there is a chance she can work the obstruction out herself.

Question 98: You have been unsuccessful in starting an IV on a 2 year old child that is in cardiac arrest. Your medical direction indicates you should consider initiating IO access to administer medications. As you prepare this procedure what are the anatomical landmarks you are looking for, and what are the complication risks with this procedure?

b. proximal tibia / pulmonary embolism

Rationale: The proximal tibia is the usual site to establish an IO catheter in a pediatric patient. All of the above mentioned complication risks are correct. Fracture of the tibia, pulmonary embolism, compartment syndrome, and severe pain upon infusion of fluids can be possible when initiating IO access.

Question 99: Which set contains parts of the lower airway only?

d. Trachea, alveoli, bronchi, and bronchioles

Rationale: The lower airway is composed of the trachea, alveoli, bronchioles, bronchi, and diaphragm.

Question 100: A DNR is?

c. An advanced directive

Rationale: Do Not Resuscitate. This is a legal document directing medical care (or refusing interventions) should the patient stop breathing or go into cardiac arrest.

Question 101: The umbilical cord is wrapped tightly around the baby's neck and you have tried unsuccessfully to slip the cord over the head. What should your next course of action be?

b. Clamp the cord in two places and cut it in the middle

Rationale: Getting the baby's airway patent is the most important thing so cutting the cord appropriately would be the best decision at this point.

Question 102: You arrive on scene to find a 78 year old man who is sitting in a chair and staring off into space. His breathing is labored and you can hear wet lung sounds. You get no answer when you try to get his name. Your requests for him to move his toes go without response. Immediate treatment for this patient would include _____.

c. High flow O2

Rationale: Oxygen is about all you can do for this patient at a basic or intermediate level. For higher level caregivers, medications like Furosemide, a diuretic, can be administered to help clear fluid in the lungs.

Question 103: If a Paramedic instructs you to hyperventilate the patient prior to intubation, what would you do?

b. Assist ventilations with 100% oxygen for several minutes

Rationale: Paramedics were taught for many years to hyperventilate (meaning to give the patient more breaths with a BVM or other artificial ventilation device) for the purpose of preparing for intubation. Research has now shown that there is only a need to pre-oxygenate the patient. You may still have paramedics use the term Hyperventilate, but understand the intent of the procedure. You don't need to ventilate faster, just provide 100% oxygen for a few minutes of normal ventilations.

The reason for doing pre-oxygenation is that it buys more time to perform the intubation. The idea is that we replace all the air in the respiratory system with 100% oxygen, and since there is about 2.4 liters of air that are in the functional reserve capacity (FRC) of the lungs (average) we are trying to turn all of it into 100% oxygen and replace all that Nitrogen that is normally present. If we do some simple math we can see how effective this is. If room air is at 21% oxygen and the FRC is 2.4 liters then there are about 500 ml of oxygen in the patient. If we replace all that 2.4 liters with 100% oxygen we now have nearly 5 times the available oxygen just sitting there. This oxygen will still diffuse into the patient while the paramedic is attempting the intubation. This gives a little bit of padding to allow the intubation and prevent the patient from becoming hypoxic.

Question 104: After the baby's head has delivered you should?

a. Suction the mouth and nose then check if the cord is wrapped around the infant's neck

Rationale: As soon as the head has exited the vagina you should suction the mouth and nose and check to see that the cord is not wrapped around the baby's neck.

Question 105: You arrive on scene to find a 57 year old man who is sitting on a couch appearing to stare at the wall. His breathing is labored and you can hear wet breath sounds that are producing a pink foam dripping from his mouth. You get no response when you try to get his name. Your requests for him to move his arm go without response. His pulse is 105 and his BP is 92/40. You do not see any edema, swelling, or JVD. This patient likely has _____.

a. Left sided CHF

Rationale: Left sided Congestive Heart Failure typically produces crackles or wet lung sounds and is accompanied by pink foamy sputum. With right sided CHF you would expect to see edema, swelling, or distended jugular veins because of the back up of fluids into the vasculature.

Question 106: You are dispatched to a home for a laceration. A 60 yr old male was chopping wood with a hatchet when he missed and hit his wrist. When you make patient contact, his wrist is still actively bleeding. Which of the following treatment sequences would be the MOST appropriate ?

c. Direct pressure - tourniquet

Rationale: The only answer that has a correct sequence of treatment is the 3rd. All other answer choices are out of order to the degree that the NREMT bleeding control/shock management practical skill sheet would have been failed. Critical criteria of "did not control hemorrhage in a timely manner". Remember, this question asks what is the MOST appropriate TREATMENT... it does not ask you to list all the steps of the bleeding control skill sheet. Elevating the wounded extremity is no longer part of the NREMT skill sheet. BSI is not included in the correct answer because it is not part of the treatment. The answer choices with BSI included, fail the critical criteria.

Question 107: A woman who is multigravida but primipara would have?

b. Had multiple pregnancies with one live birth

Rationale: Multigravida signifies that she has been pregnant multiple times and primipara means that she has had one birth. Primipara can also suggest that the mother had twins or a stillborn baby.

Question 108: Meconium is:

b. Often found in amniotic fluid when the fetus has voided in the womb.

Rationale: Meconium is the first stools of a newborn. It is a dark green tarry stool composed of water, amniotic fluid, mucus, and other materials ingested while the infant is still in the uterus. Stress and other factors can cause a fetus to have it's first bowel movement in the womb. Though nearly sterile and odorless, it can cause airway and delivery problems if not managed correctly. Bowel movements of meconium may continue for a few days after birth as the child finishes digesting.

Question 109: A 6 year old girl was found outside in her yard unconscious. She is breathing 6 breaths a minute and her pulse is 58 bpm with poor systematic perfusion. What should you do?

b. Initiate chest compressions and assist ventilations with high flow O2

Rationale: AHA Guidelines for BLS include compressions for children with a pulse rate of less than 60 bpm who are perfusing poorly. Symptomatic bradycardia is a common terminal rhythm in infants and children. Don't wait for pulseless arrest to begin compressions.

Question 110: Anaphylaxis may involve more than one of the body's systems. Which of the following systems are involved?

c. Respiratory and neurological

Rationale: While each answer contains a correct answer, the reproductive system is not involved in anaphylaxis.

Question 111: Your 34 year old patient is breathing on their own at a rate of 18 per minute and an approximate tidal volume of 150 mL. What should you do?

b. Give positive pressure ventilations with high flow O2

Rationale: A patient who is only breathing with a tidal volume of 150 mL is ineffective at oxygenating the tissues at any rate. The reason is that approximately 150 mL of air resides in the dead space of the airway and never reaches the alveoli. If the patient is only taking in 150 mL, the oxygen is never reaching the alveoli. This is conversely true with carbon dioxide being expelled from the lungs.

Question 112: In order to speed delivery of the placenta the EMS provider should?

d. Let the placenta deliver on its own

Rationale: None of the above is recommended and all of the other answers can be dangerous. Letting the placenta deliver in it's own time is recommended (usually in 30 minutes).

Question 113: Dispatch has reported a man down near a local laundromat. The reporting party says the man is "breathing very fast , but not very deep." The reporting party also says that, "The man has stopped breathing several times, but then begins breathing fast again." What is the most likely cause of this man's respiratory pattern?

a. Somebody hit him in the head with a hammer

Rationale: This breathing pattern is referred to as Biot's or "cluster breathing/respirations", it is indicative of a head wound and injury to the medulla oblongata. Can also be caused by strokes and uncal or tentorial herniations.

Question 114: You and your partner Tom arrive on scene of a gang shooting where the police have secured the area. There are two patients in their teens with multiple gunshot wounds to the arms, legs, and chest. You would immediately?

d. Apply 3-sided dressing to the chest wounds and assess breathing while your partner treats the other patient

Rationale: A gunshot wound to the chest is a life threatening injury and should be treated immediately with a 3-sided dressing as long as the scene is safe (the scenario said it was). The other answers may have things that should be done but not immediately.

Question 115: When assessing the breathing of an infant or child, you should look for_____?

c. Presence or absence of breathing

Rationale: AHA Guidelines specify that with children, you should verify the presence or absence of breathing. Also ALS continues to look for adequate breathing.

Question 116: You and your partner Gene respond to a report of a car vs. pedestrian. An elderly man has been struck by a car and is now on the sidewalk lying supine. Gene takes C-spine and you begin an initial assessment noticing that the man's breathing is fast and very shallow. He does not respond to you and also has some liquid or vomit running from his mouth. The best choice of action would be?

c. Suction his mouth

Rationale: If he has vomit or fluid in his mouth, you do not have a patent airway and you will need to suction it BEFORE putting in an OPA. Using a BVM without the suction could possibly force vomit or liquid into his lungs. Additionally, using a BVM is moving to the Breathing step of the initial assessment before opening the airway.

Question 117: A pediatric patient may need additional measures to maintain an open airway. Which of the following is an acceptable method to use?

a. Insert an oral or nasal airway adjunct

Rationale: The only answer that is acceptable, is to utilize an oral or nasal airway adjunct. A rolled up towel (1 inch high) could be used under the shoulders, NOT the neck. The Trendelenburg position with high flow O2 will not aid in keeping the airway open. Magill forceps would not be the best choice for displacing the tongue.

Question 118: You and your partner Amy arrive on scene to find a woman with hives over much of her body. She is wheezing and complaining of difficulty breathing. Her husband says she was stung by a hornet and has no prior history of allergies. What would be the best course of action?

d. High flow O2 and rapid transportation if the patient appears to be going into anaphylaxis.

Rationale: Tending to the patient's ABC's and monitoring vitals is important in determining the onset of an anaphylactic reaction. If you administer epinephrine you would not have the patient sign a transport refusal. If you administer care, the patient needs to be transported. You do not need to make sure her BP is over 100 mmHg (that is for nitro). Having vital signs within normal limits is not a necessary criteria for giving epinephrine.

Question 119: You have a responsive patient who is able to answer your questions. What do you do?

a. History, secondary assessment, vitals

Rationale: With any patient, you should attempt to obtain a history first, and then a secondary assessment based on that information, followed by baseline vitals. This is the route of assessment as detailed by the NES.

Question 120: A call has come in from an indoor amusement park for an allergic reaction. A 16 yr old boy was eating lunch when he ingested a cookie that had small pieces of peanut baked into it. You arrive to find the boy in obvious respiratory stress with swelling and cyanosis around his lips. What would be your best course of action?_____ Why is this boy hypoperfusing?

d. Give the patient an injection of epinephrine via auto injector - His vasculature is dilated and fluid is leaking from his vessels

Rationale: The best course of action would be to address the immediate life threat, that is the airway compromise caused by the anaphylaxis. Definitive treatment for anaphylaxis is epinephrine injected intramuscularly at a 90 degree angle. (EMT B units carry epi in many areas AND it IS an NREMT basic skill). During anaphylactic shock the vessels dilate and fluid leaks from the vessels into the body's tissues, resulting in swelling and urticaria.

Question 121: A 73 year old female was in her backyard gardening when she collapsed to the ground. Her husband told 911 that "she is breathing very fast and will not talk to me." You arrive to find the woman lying on her side in the grass. She is breathing at 7 breaths per minute and her pulse is irregular and very thready. Her lungs also present with crackles upon auscultation As you are taking a blood pressure (88/66) the husband tells you that the woman has been having jaw pain and some weakness for approximately 3 days. What is the most likely cause of this woman's condition and how would you treat her?

c. Cardiogenic shock, Assist ventilations, and transport

Rationale: This woman is likely experiencing pump failure and she is hypoperfusing. Her poor respiration rate necessitates assisted ventilations. Transporting in the Fowler's would not be appropriate as it would increase the work load on the heart. Gravity increases the difficulty of pumping blood to the brain when the head and chest are elevated.

Question 122: Which of the following patients has adequate respirations?

b. A 31 year old man breathing at 20 per minute and slightly irregular

Rationale: Even though the 31 year old is breathing slightly irregular, they are within range and considered adequate. The 10 year old, although he may be just inside the top limit of respirations, is not breathing adequately because of the accessory muscle use.

Question 123: According to the current AHA Guidelines how many milliliters of tidal volume should you deliver via BVM to an adult patient who is apneic?

d. Just enough to give adequate chest rise

Rationale: According to AHA Guidelines you should give just enough volume to cause adequate chest rise. Studies showed it was difficult, if not impossible, to estimate the tidal volume in ml. On a side note, The AHA recommends configuring all CPR manikins to 500ml-600ml.

Question 124: If a person has dyspnea what is happening?

b. They are having trouble breathing

Rationale: Problems breathing is termed dyspnea. Dys refers to difficulty and pnea refers to breathing.

Question 125: You are called to a youth summer camp for a 12 year old girl having difficulty breathing. En route to the camp you are told that a group of kids were having lunch when a hive of bees was disturbed near by. The kids took off running and when they stopped the patient began having a hard time breathing. She has no known allergies. What is the best course of action?

b. Ask the girl if she is choking. Initiate treatment and immediate transport in a position of comfort.

Rationale: Before you initiate any treatment for this patient you will want to confirm the cause of the breathing difficulty if you can. Just because there are bees present do not assume that she is going into anaphalaxis. The kids were having lunch and there is a good chance that the girl has an airway obstruction caused by food. Do not put an oxygen mask on a patient who has a possible FBAO as it may excacerbate the respiratory problems.

Question 126: A woman with preeclampsia will _____.

a. Have swelling in the feet, hands, and or face

Rationale: This condition can result in seizures and coma and is very dangerous. The patient has extreme swelling in the extremities and high blood pressure.

Question 127: You and your partner Steve arrive at an apartment building where you are greeted outside by a very upset woman. She says her husband is upstairs and needs help. He is a 57 year old and was a chain smoker for 35 years. As you enter the apartment, the man is sitting in a tripod position and pursing his lips while exhaling. Why is this patient pursing his lips?

d. To keep alveoli open with back pressure

Rationale: Breathing with pursed lips is a sign that a COPD patient is trying to keep the alveoli open by creating back pressure on their lungs.

Question 128: You arrive on scene at a single-car accident involving a moose. Your patient was driving about 50 MPH when she hit the moose. After completing your scene size up, to which of the following would you proceed?

c. The patient's chief complaint

Rationale: According to the NREMT Patient Assessment /Management - Trauma Skill sheet, you would want to proceed with the primary survey. This begins with verbalizing a general impression of the patient, determining level of consciousness, and determining the chief complaint and apparant life threats. Baseline vital signs would not be taken until after the secondary assessment. A detailed physical exam (secondary assessment) would not be completed until the primary survey is finished. A SAMPLE history would not be taken until the primary survey is completed and a transport decision was made.

Question 129: Incident Command has made you transportation officer at a multiple casualty incident. A walking bridge at a nearby park has collapsed and there were 10-20 people on the bridge suffering varying degrees of injuries. You have two hospitals at your disposal. Santa Cruz Hospital is 3 miles away and Valley Hospital is 15 miles away. Which of the following transportation choices would be the BEST?

a. Send all the red tagged patients to Santa Cruz until they are at capacity. Then send any remaining red tagged patients to Valley Hospital followed by yellow and green tagged patients.

Rationale: Among all the choices, the most appropriate would be to send the priority one (red) patients to the nearest hospital, and the less priority patients (yellow and green) to the hospital further away. This can be altered based on the need of a specialized treatment center. For example: If you have a yellow tagged pediatric patient, and the closest hospital is the pediatric center.

Question 130: You arrive on scene of a one-car motor vehicle accident. A single female patient can be observed in the car having breathing difficulties. You notice power lines are down across the hood of the car but you do not see any sparks. What would be your best course of action?

b. Notify the power company and keep a safe distance until they have removed the wires

Rationale: You need to be positive the scene is safe. Remember, the absence of sparks does not mean the wires are not charged. You should never approach a vehicle that has power lines over it until you are assured by the utility company that there is no risk for electric shock.

Question 131: A person who is in anaphylaxis will have blood vessels that are _____.

b. Dilated

Rationale: A person in anaphylaxis will have dilated vessels which will cause a drop in blood pressure. The dilation is caused by a mediator release of histamine which causes among other things, smooth muscle tone in the blood vessels.

Question 132: You have just delivered a quartet of quadruplets. Q1 has pale blue arms and legs. His pulse is 100 and he is breathing at about 50 breaths per minute. Q2 has a pulse of 130, a respiratory rate of 40, and core cyanosis. Q3 has core cyanosis, a pulse of 60 beats per minute, and a respiratory rate of 30. Q4 is breathing at around 30 breaths per minute. Her pulse is about 110 beats per minute and she has peripheral cyanosis. To which of these children are you going to give CPR?

c. Q3

Rationale: Q1 has peripheral cyanosis, but he has a good pulse and good respirations which can quickly eliminate the afore mentioned cyanosis. Q2 has a good pulse, a good respiratory rate, and core cyanosis which can be overcome with good vitals and stimulation. Q3 has inadequate respiratory rate and function, a pulse that is too slow to give adequate perfusion, and an appearance that is poor with the central cyanosis. This child should be given CPR. Q4 has a respiratory rate that is a little slow, but her pulse is good. The peripheral cyanosis may be overcome with tactile stimulation and drying.

Question 133: Proper use of an AED should include:

c. Establishing the patient does not have a pulse

Rationale: An AED should only be used on a patient who has no pulse. CPR should be continued after each shock, per the 2010 AHA Guidelines.

Question 134: You and your partner answer the call for a 1-year-old boy who was dropped on his head by his older brother. His mother said he hit his head on the edge of the coffee table on the way down. You would not expect which of the following?

c. Sunken fontanelles

Rationale: It is true that head injuries are more prevalent in children because their heads are larger in proportion to their bodies. When assessing the head injury of a child you should check for bleeding, swelling, bruising, and hematomas. The fontanelle will actually depress when a child is dehydrated, and swell with a head injury where there is intracranial bleeding or pressure.

Question 135: A train derailment has caused two tanker cars to explode and several others to begin leaking an unknown gas. The size of the affected area is large and crosses several county lines. According to NIMS, this type of MCI would benefit most from a:

b. Unified Command System

Rationale: Unified Command Systems can involve many different agencies such as EMS, Fire Departments, Law Enforcment, City Managers, County Commisioners, etc.

Question 136: You arrive on scene with your partner Ebstein to find a man in his 50's who is staggering around outside of a casino with blood trickling down his face from a laceration on his head. He complies when you ask him to sit down and he maintains eye contact with you while you ask him questions. You ask him what his name is and he slurs "nibralizxsnafrb". You ask him what day it is and he again slurs "kbmefrolzx". Your partner Ebstein, an expert in linguistics, assures you that what you are hearing is not another language. This patient has a GCS of what?

a. 12

Rationale: He gets a 4 for the good eye contact and a 6 for obeying the command to sit down. He gets a 2 for words that are incomprehensible, for a total of 12.

Question 137: You and your partner Monte are transporting a 4 year old child who has ingested some oven cleaner. The mother insists on holding the child during transport. In the best interest of the patient and parent you should?

b. Explain the reasons quickly why she may not hold the child and secure the child to the stretcher

Rationale: You should not let a parent hold a child in the back of a moving ambulance. It is best for treatment and for safety.

Question 138: You are the first EMS unit on scene of a multiple casualty incident. A crane has fallen from a building roof top and ripped through an adjacent building. What should you do according to the ICS?

d. Take incident command until relieved or reassigned

Rationale: If you are the first EMS personnel on scene you should inform dispatch that you are the IC until notified differently. Once other personnel arrive on scene, you may be reassigned to triage, transportation, treatment, or logistics.

Question 139: You and your partner Greg are called to a hockey arena where a fan was struck in the side of the chest with a hockey puck that was hit over the protective glass and into the crowd. The man is having a painful time breathing at about 16 a minute. He says his ribs really hurt. What should your treatment include?

b. High flow O2 via NRB and rapid transport

Rationale: As long as the patient is able to talk and keep their respirations within range, then high flow O2 and transport would be your best choice.

Question 140: You and your partner whom you have been working with for two years are called to a house where a woman is having chest pain and complaining of shortness of breath. She is diaphoretic and has a pulse of 110, respirations of 22, and a blood pressure of 140/80. She says she has no cardiac or respiratory history. You should?

c. Perform your assessment, put her on O2 at 15 lpm, and transport

Rationale: The best thing you could do in this case is to give her oxygen and get her to the hospital.

Question 141: Dispatch has called you to the scene of a possible drowning. You and your partner Efron arrive on scene to find two people giving mouth to mouth to a 50ish male. "I am a doctor," announces one of the rescuers, "...he has a good strong pulse but was not breathing when we pulled him from the water." After re-opening the patient's airway and hooking up the bag valve mask, you begin ventilating the patient at _____. Each respiratory cycle should last approximately _____ with a tidal volume of _____.

b. 10-12 breaths per minute / 5-6 seconds / enough to cause adequate chest rise

Rationale: Proper artificial ventilation rates for an adult are 10-12 breaths per minute. Don't confuse it with the normal breathing rate of 12-20 in an adult. Additionally, the artificial ventilation rate for children is 12-20 (and their normal respiration rate is 20-30). Tidal volume is now measured by "adequate chest rise" and not by a specific numeric volume.

Question 142: A motor vehicle accident has occurred right in front of your ambulance and requires the patients to be extricated. Your first choice of location to accomplish the rapid extrication should be the?

d. The door

Rationale: Always check all of the doors before cutting through the car with the Jaws of Life. One will often be able to extricate the patient through a door that can be opened.

Question 143: You are called to the scene of a 35 year old woman in labor. Dispatch tells you that the baby's arm is sticking out of the vagina. You should be prepared to?

d. Cover the arm and vagina with a moist, sterile dressing and transport rapidly

Rationale: You should never push anything back into the vagina. This type of birth requires definitive care. Transport with a moist sterile cloth is the best choice.

Question 144: Your patient is a 69 year old female who has a history of diabetes. She is breathing very deeply and very rapidly in a state of respiratory acidosis. Her husband said he woke up to her breathing like this and she would not wake up. You know that this woman is most likely in?

b. A diabetic coma

Rationale: A diabetic coma will often present with the patient breathing deeply and rapidly. The body is trying to blow off the build up of ketones(acids).

Question 145: What will Epinephrine do if administered per auto injector?

c. Dilate the bronchial passages and constrict the vessels of the circulatory system

Rationale: Epi will dilate the bronchial passages and constrict the vessels of the circulatory system, easing the breathing difficulty and processing the allergen.

Question 146: Without knowing anything else, what condition would you say the following patient is in? A 30 year old male with a pulse rate of 40, breathing at 10 breaths per minute, and a systolic BP of 90.

b. Poor

Rationale: A patient who has bradycardia (HR less than 60), slow respirations (below 12), and a systolic BP of less than

100 would most likely be in a very poor condition.

Question 147: You and your partner Willy have just arrived at a restaurant where a man has fallen through a glass door. He has a laceration across his lower leg approximately 10 inches long and 1.5 inches deep. Which of the following treatment sequences would be the MOST appropriate?

b. Apply pressure to the wound - Elevate the legs - Transport

Rationale: The only answer that has a correct sequence of treatment is the 2nd. The other answer choices are out of order and would cause failure of the critical criteria of the NREMT bleeding control/shock management practical skill sheet (Did not control hemorrhage in a timely manner). BSI is not included in the correct answer because it is not part of the treatment. The answer choices with BSI included fail the critical criteria. NOTE: Elevating the extremity is no longer part of skill sheet however, elevating the legs is for treatment of shock.

Question 148: Your patient has been kicked in the chest by a horse and is having trouble breathing. Lung sounds are non existent on the right side where she was kicked and you believe she has a tension pneumothorax. During inhalation, her _____ _____ impeding ventilation. When she exhales, her _____ _____.

b. mediastinum moves left / mediastinum shifts, distorting the vena cava which results in poor venous return

Rationale: With a tension pneumothorax, you would expect the blood pressure to drop, not rise, as venous return is inhibited by the shifting of the mediastinum and distoration of the vena cava. During a pneumothorax, the pleural space fills with air from a hole in the lungs. Not the other way around.

Question 149: Your patient is a 14 year old girl who is complaining of vaginal pain after falling onto the center post of her bike. She is alone and very scared. She has called the accident in on her cell phone and stated that she is bleeding very badly and feeling faint. Besides treating for shock, what other things should you consider with this patient?

d. Having a female EMT respond for the patient's modesty

Rationale: Having a female EMT respond out of concern for the patient's modesty would be a good consideration. Unfortunately, having a female EMT is not always possible.

Question 150: Gastric distention can interfere with movement of the diaphragm and lead to what other problem?

a. Hypoventilation

Rationale: When the diaphragm cannot move very well, that inhibits breathing. Poor breathing will lead to low oxygen levels or hypoxia.

Question 151: Changes during pregnancy usually include _____.

d. Increase in plasma volume

Rationale: Changes would be a lower blood pressure, increase in plasma volume, increase in blood volume, lowering of blood pressure, and increase in heart rate.

Question 152: Your patient is the victim of a moderate speed MVA. The patient is unconscious and not breathing. You attempt to open their airway with a jaw thrust maneuver and are unsuccessful. What should you do next?

a. Use the head tilt chin lift maneuver

Rationale: AHA Guidelines state that after an unsuccessful attempt at opening the patient's airway with the jaw thrust maneuver, you should use the head tilt chin lift maneuver. Opening the airway is priority.

Question 153: You suspect a significant mechanism of injury. In what order would you conduct the assessment?

c. Primary survey, SAMPLE history, rapid full-body scan

Rationale: The National EMS Education Standard details that assessment be done in the following order: Scene size-up, primary survey/primary assessment, history taking, secondary assessment (of which a Rapid full-body scan and vital signs are included), and reassessment.

Question 154: An unconscious patient would give what type of consent?

a. Implied

Rationale: If they were unconscious it would be implied because they would not be able to communicate with you.

Question 155: You arrive on scene to find an 11 year old girl who was struck by a truck while riding her bike. She is unresponsive to painful stimuli and has a large abrasion on her left side. She is breathing at 24 respirations per minute and regular. Your next course of action would be?

a. C-spine precautions and Administer high flow O2 with an NRB

Rationale: Her respirations are within range and she was just struck by a car. C-spine precautions and high flow oxygen would be the best choice.

Question 156: You are standing by at a local sporting event when a mother rushes up to you with a 3 year old boy in her arms. " He was playing with my car keys and then just started gagging and coughing!", she tells you in a panic. The child is having difficulty breathing and crying along with audible inspiratory stridor. What should you do?

d. Give blow by oxygen and carefully monitor during transport.

Rationale: As long as the child is able to pass an adequate amount of air, which this child appears to be doing, then supportive care, transport, and oxygen therapy is all that should be done. Complete occlusion of the airway would obviously necessitate different measures.

Question 157: You arrive on scene with your partner Abe to find a 64 year old woman who is very obese. Her son tells you she has a heart condition. She is unconscious with a baggie of what appears to be street drugs next to her. She is breathing at 18 breaths a minute and they are regular. Her pulse is 99 and her BP is 90/50. What is likely the cause for the low blood pressure?

c. The drugs

Rationale: Drugs and shock should be considered with an unconscious patient who has a low blood pressure. All other signs in this woman would point to high blood pressure, were it not for the drug potential.

Question 158: Anatomical differences in a child's respiratory system can make opening and maintaining the airway a difficult and challenging process. Which of the following choices correctly states some of the problems and solutions associated with these anatomical differences?

c. A child's tongue is larger and takes up considerably more room in the mouth. Using a tongue depressor to hold the tongue down while inserting an OPA without rotating it will be more effective than techniques used in adults.

Rationale: A child's larynx sits more ANTERIOR and superior. Put a towel under the child's shoulders NOT the head. The pharynx in a child is SMALLER. The cricoid ring is SMALLER. Do not insert suction into the cricoid.

Question 159: You have just arrived on scene with your partner Ellen to a call. It's a 75 year old man with chest pain. He has already taken 1 nitro tablet, but the pain persists. What should you do?

d. Ask him if he takes any erectile dysfunction drugs and take his BP

Rationale: You need to verify his pressure is not too low to take nitro and of course if it is his and the date is good. You would not withhold oxygen from this patient.

Question 160: It is the middle of winter and you and your partner are called to the scene of a homeless man having breathing problems. You arrive to find him laying on a sidewalk on a calm, but very cold night. He is likely losing heat from?

a. Conduction

Rationale: The cold pavement is likely conducting the heat away from his body. While there could be evaporation and convection at play, both of those options are less of an impact than someone who is in contact with cold concrete.

Question 161: Which of the following is considered a sign?

b. There is blood in the vomit of the patient

Rationale: A sign is any medical or trauma assessment finding that can be seen, felt, or heard by the provider. A symptom is any medical or trauma condition that is described to the provider by the patient.

Question 162: Which of the following would be the best indication that a patient is suffering from hypoxia?

b. Their oxygen saturation is 87% while you have them on O2 at 15 LPM

Rationale: Breathing shallow and fast is not a good indicator. Cool and moist on their own is not enough and rapid pulse and pale skin are not enough. A factual SpO2 sat would give you the best information.

Question 163: You arrive on scene to find a woman in her 20's who phoned in her own diabetic emergency. She is now unconscious and breathing at 20 a minute with a pulse of 110. She told the dispatcher on the phone that she had hypoglycemia and had not eaten that day. Your best course of treatment would include?

d. Obtain a blood sugar, O2 via NRB at 15 lpm, and Initiate an IV of D5W

Rationale: Administering D5 via IV would be the best choice from the options given.

Question 164: You are assessing a patient who is complaining of severe chest pain. They are sweating and their BP is 96/55. You have their medications with you and they include a prescription for nitroglycerin. You contact medical control and they order you to give the patient 1 nitro tablet sublingually. What would you do?

a. Repeat the blood pressure and ask again what they would like you to do

Rationale: Giving nitroglycerin to someone who has a systolic blood pressure below 100 is likely to cause it to go dangerously low and is not advised. Assuming responsibility and liability for your decision to decline is another issue for you to think about.

Question 165: You are transporting an unconscious but breathing 55 year old male who has suffered a head injury. He has an oropharyngeal airway in place. You hear gurgling sounds during his respirations and you need to suction his airway. How should this be accomplished?

c. By inserting the catheter and suctioning until the airway is clear

Rationale: You do not want to deprive the patient of oxygen for a prolonged period however, you must remove the obstruction in order for the patient to be ventilated.

Question 166: A child between 3-5 would have normal vitals if they were?

d. 20 breaths a minute, pulse of 100, and Systolic BP of 110

Rationale: A child between 3 and 5 (preschool-age) should have respirations between 20-30, a pulse of 80-120, and a systolic BP of 80 - 110.

Question 167: A 45 year old male patient is complaining of headaches and fatigue. He has had a fever of over 102 degrees for 3 days now and he says his neck hurts when he moves his head around. These signs and symptoms make you consider that this man is suffering from?

c. Meningitis

Rationale: Persistent headache, fatigue, fever, and neck pain are all classic signs of meningitis.

Question 168: You and your partner Mark arrive on scene to find a 35 year old man who is slurring his speech. He shows positive for left arm drift and the left side of his face is drooping slightly when he tries to speak. How should this patient be transported?

a. On their left side

Rationale: A patient who is showing signs of a stroke should be transported with the affected side down, with the head elevated about 6 inches.

Question 169: You are the Incident Commander at the scene of a bus rollover. A tourist group of approximately 25 senior citizens was on the bus when it overturned on a sharp corner. Which of the following actions would be appropriate?

c. Assigning a triage officer, treatment officer, and a transportation officer

Rationale: Part of the Incident Commander's responsibilities can be to assign different officers to manage the different components of the ICS. This includes triage, treatment, and transportation of the patients. The IC would not likely be physically helping with extrication as they would then not have command of the other ICS components.

Question 170: You and your partner Rob arrive on scene to find a woman in her 37th week of pregnancy. She says that she feels like she is ready to give birth and asks you to take her to the hospital. While Rob takes vital signs in route, you are assessing how far along the woman is. She has some hemorrhaging from the vaginal opening which makes you think that she may have _____ or _____.

c. Placenta previa or placenta abruptio

Rationale: Placenta abruptio is when the placenta prematurely separates from the wall of the uterus. Placenta previa is when the placenta is blocking the cervix and presenting before the baby. They are best managed by transporting the patient on their left side to prevent supine hypotension.

Question 171: Which of the following is a high priority condition?

b. Severe pain

Rationale: Uncomplicated childbirth is not a high priority condition. Severe pain anywhere is high priority.

Question 172: You are assessing an 83 year old woman who has COPD and CHF. She is sitting upright in her chair and appears to understand that you are an EMT here to help her. You should?

c. Be honest with the patient about her conditions

Rationale: You want to make eye contact and address the person by Mr. or Mrs. Rather than terms of endearment like "honey" or "dear". You should try to be at eye level or slightly below for best communication.

Question 173: Nitroglycerin has what affect on the body's vessels?

a. Dilation to ease the preload on heart

Rationale: Nitro dilates the vessels and relieves the heart of some of the preload on the heart.

Question 174: Which breath sounds would you likely hear from a person whose alveoli contain fluid?

a. Crackles

Rationale: Lungs that contain fluid will present with crackles.

Question 175: With regard to the airway and breathing of a child, which of the following statements is most accurate?

c. Use of a pediatric resuscitation tape can aid in the selection of the correct equipment

Rationale: The only answer that is correct is utilizing a PED tape to choose the correct equipment. A towel should be used to help align the airway, but it should be used under the shoulders NOT the neck. Airway adjuncts are fine to use in children and are in fact recommended. If a child is using accessory muscles they are not likely breathing adequately.

Question 176: Which of the following is a rare cause of respiratory failure in children?

d. Croup

Rationale: Croup is a relatively common condition that affects about 15% of children at some point, most often between 6 months and 5-6 years of age. The other choices are dire emergencies that can lead to respiratory failure and require immediate care and transport.

Question 177: Your patient is an 86 year old female who is complaining of difficulty breathing. She says it has been getting worse for the last few hours. She has a cough that she says, "has been..(breath) a companion(breath) for years." During your assessment you find that she has a rapid pulse and diminished breath sounds on her right side. She also says her chest hurts every time she coughs. What is the likely cause of this woman's complaint?

b. Pneumothorax

Rationale: This woman likely has COPD, but the absence of breath sounds and the pain when she coughs is a sign that she has a spontaneous pneumothorax. Pulmonary Effusions is a made up term (it's pulmonary EMBOLISM and Pleural Effusion). People with weakened lung tissue can cough and cause a spontaneous pneumothorax.

Question 178: Using lights and sirens during a cardiac arrest transport is?

c. A consideration for moving quickly and safely through traffic

Rationale: Using lights and sirens should have a purpose. Sometimes it is the last thing in the world you want. Using lights and sirens to safely and quickly expedite a patient is acceptable and expected.

Question 179: You and your partner Naven have just arrived at a home where a woman in her 70's was reported to have passed out. You enter the residence to find a man in his 20's performing rescue breathing on the elderly woman who is supine on the floor. Naven attaches the AED and advises the man to move away. He pushes the analyze button and no shock is advised. The two of you begin CPR, delivering approximately_____. After 1 cycle of CPR an elderly gentleman enters the room and shows you a valid looking DNR signed by the patient and her doctor. What should you do?_____

b. 6 breaths and 110 compressions over 1 minute / Respect the DNR

Rationale: AHA Guidelines specify that a 30:2 compression to ventilation ratio be used during CPR on this patient. The ratio would yield approximately 6 breaths per minute and at least compressions. On the second part of the question: If someone shows you a valid DNR you should respect it and discontinue resuscitation.

Question 180: An intervention for someone who is apneic would be _____.

d. All of the above

Rationale: Anything done to make the situation better for the patient would be considered an intervention. All of these interventions would be for a non-breathing patient.

Question 181: You and your partner Loni arrive on scene to find 4 patients. Which one of them would be your priority?

c. A 7 year old who is conscious, with respirations of 27, and a systolic of 68 mm Hg

Rationale: The key to this answer is knowing that a child with a blood pressure lower than 70 mm Hg is considered critical. A patient this age should have a systolic around 100.

Question 182: The National Incident Management System (NIMS) includes a componant referred to as "Interoperability". This componant is concerned with:

c. Communication between EMS, fire and law enforcement during an MCI.

Rationale: Interoperability is an important issue for law enforcement, fire fighting, EMS, and other public health and safety departments, because first responders need to be able to communicate during wide-scale emergencies.

Question 183: You are dispatched to a report of a breathing difficulty. Upon arrival, you find a 67 year old female patient who appears to be tired, but responds to your questioning. Her husband reports that she appeared to have trouble breathing when he came home. She reports that she has been progressively becoming more short of breath as the day has progressed. She has a history of breast cancer and a fractured left tibia. You assess her vitals and they reveal a blood pressure of 68/50, pulse of 80, and respiratory rate of 32. Her oxygen saturation is 79% on her home cannula at 2 lpm. Your next step in the care of this patient should include?

a. High flow oxygen via NRB, consider rapid transport

Rationale: Due to her blood pressure and stated complaint, the patient should be a high priority. She should be placed on an NRB with high flow oxygen.

Question 184: The structure of an incident command system:

b. Can contain multiple sectors, but only one incident commander

Rationale: The structure of an ICS can be broken down into several different sectors from EMS, Fire, Hazmat, Extrication etc. Different officers may be appointed to lead each sector of the operation. It is very effective.

Question 185: Which patient is most viable?

d. 5 y/o who fell through the ice and was submerged for 10 minutes before being brought to your ambulance. She is not breathing and doesn't have a pulse.

Rationale: Drowning victims should be treated even if they have been submerged for a long time. The rule "no patient should be pronounced dead until warm and dead" applies. Children in particular have a good chance of survival in water up to 3 minutes, or 10 minutes in cold water (10 to 15 °C or 50 to 60 °F). The infant has rigor mortis and should not be worked. The DNR negates the need to begin CPR on the elderly patient. The 38 y/o male has suffered major trauma, and while all efforts will be given, the odds of surviving a traumatic arrest are very small.

Question 186: What is the area of hazardous contamination known as?

c. Hot zone

Rationale: An area of contamination is referred to as the hot zone.

Question 187: After applying a cervical collar to a patient and securing them to the backboard what must you check before transporting them?

b. Their CMS

Rationale: You need to check their pulse and motor sensory function after making the intervention of applying the collar.

Question 188: You arrive on scene with your partner to a call of "man down". You pull into the driveway of the house in a very exclusive part of town. In the driveway a man is lying face up with his eyes closed. After making sure the scene is safe, what actions will help you gather the most information in the shortest period of time?

d. Check his pulse with your hand while you put your ear near his mouth and look down at the sternum for chest rise

Rationale: You need to determine his level of responsiveness, assess his pulse, and see whether or not he is breathing. This would be best achieved with the 4th answer.

Question 189: You are called to a scene of a 3-year-old who is not breathing and is pulseless. Your CPR should include compressions at what depth?

c. At least 1/3rd the depth of the chest

Rationale: 2010 AHA guidelines stipulate that at least 1/3rd of the anterior posterior diameter of the chest should be compressed while performing CPR on a child.

Question 190: You arrive on scene with your partner Leonard to the report of a child appearing lethargic. Upon entering the house, you see a 9-year-old girl lying on the couch. Her father says she has been breathing strangely and began vomiting about 45 minutes ago. During your assessment, you determine she needs to be transported to the ER immediately. Which of the following sets of vitals would lead you to believe this girl is in need of immediate transport?

b. BP 100/58, respirations of 14 per minute and a pulse of 130

Rationale: The second answer is the set of vitals that would warrant immediate transport. The respirations are too slow and the pulse is too fast. All other options fall within the normal range for this age of patient.

Question 191: During one person CPR you can assess ventilations by watching what?

a. Bilateral rise and fall of the chest

Rationale: Watching rise and fall of the chest is the most reliable way of verifying ventilations among the choices.

Question 192: You are called to a neighborhood pool where a 5 year old girl was found floating unconscious. She is cyanotic and has no muscle tone. Your partner Greg does not find a pulse and the child is not breathing. Your CPR should include a compression to ventilation ratio of_____ and each compression should be at a depth of_____.

b. 15:2 / one third of the anterior-posterior diameter of the chest

Rationale: 2010 AHA CPR Guidelines specify that 2 person CPR by health care professionals should be done at a 15:2 ratio. Each chest compression should be 1/3 of the anterior-posterior diameter of the chest. These numbers are argued by more EMT AND Paramedic candidates than any other question type we have. Please refer to your 2010 AHA CPR for Healthcare Provider guidelines.

Question 193: Why would inserting a suction catheter into the mouth with the suction active be incorrect?

c. It depletes the patient's oxygen supply

Rationale: You will deplete the patient's oxygen supply. This is the only logical reason.

Question 194: You are driving an ambulance with lights and sirens going when you approach a busy 4 way stop. The car stopped to your right appears to acknowledge that your ambulance is responding to an emergency. As you continue through the intersection the car pulls out in front of you and you collide with the driver's side door. Who is at fault and why?

a. You the ambulance driver is at fault because you did not stop, slow down or use due regard at the intersection

Rationale: While right of way privileges are different from state to state you the ambulance driver are at fault for not stopping, slowing down or using due regard. Even if your state allows you to proceed through a controlled intersection using due regard, not slowing down or stopping in this situation would be considered the absents of due regard.

Question 195: Which type of shock would you suspect to find in a patient who has vomiting, urinating, and diarrhea?

d. Hypovolemic shock

Rationale: Hypovolemic shock can result from excessive vomiting, urination, and diarrhea as the body voids much of the fluids that is needed to balance itself. This may also cause changes in the bodies metabolic balance and need further care to balance the metabolic system as well.

Question 196: Two ambulances are proceeding together toward a scene and are approaching an intersection where the traffic light is currently green. You are the driver of the second ambulance. Which of the following choices describes the best method for proceeding through the intersection?

d. use a different siren tone than the one the first ambulance is using and consider slowing down to look for pedestrians or other cars as the light may change.

Rationale: Intersections are the most common place for an ambulance crash to happen. Regardless of the right of way privileges in your state you must use due regard for the safety of others. Erroring on the side of caution and slowing down at the intersection would be showing due regard Two emergency vehicles moving together poses additional safety concerns because a pedestrian or driver may not anticipate more than one vehicle. A car may yield the right of way to the first vehicle and then proceed through the intersection or turn in front of the second emergency vehicle. Using a different siren tone can help drivers make the distinction that there are two (or more) emergency vehicles moving together. There is no data that suggests it will make drivers believe that the vehicles are appoaching from different directions.

Question 197: You have responded to a request for transportation of a female patient in her 37th week of pregnancy. You arrive to find the woman in active labor with contractions less than 2 minutes apart. The baby is crowning. What are you going to do?

a. BSI, Apply gentle, supportive pressure to the baby's head and mother's perineum to prevent explosive delivery. Check for nucal cord as the head emerges. Suction the baby's mouth and then nose. Guide the baby's head

downward to facilitate delivery of the first shoulder and then upward to deliver the other shoulder.

Rationale: Answer 2 is not correct because you do not want to put direct pressure on the fontenelle as it may damage the baby's head. Additionally, you want to suction the baby's mouth first and then the nose, as suctioning the nose will stimulate breathing and can lead to aspiration of the contents in the oropharynx. Also, you should guide the baby's head downward first for delivery of the shoulder and then upward to help with the other one. Answer 3 is incorrect because you apply gentle pressure to the baby's head and mother's perineum as a preventative measure against an explosive delivery. Don't just wait for the head to fully emerge on it's own. Additionally, you would check for nucal cord first and then suction the mouth and the nose to help prevent aspiration of the contents in the mouth. Newborns are nose breathers and suction of the nose may stimulate the breathing reflex while the mouth is still filled with fluid. Answer 4 misses several steps and incorrectly recommends clamping the cord at the newborn's umbilicus rather than 4+ inches away.

Question 198: Your patient is a 2-year-old child. He is in respiratory distress and you have identified the need for oxygen therapy. Why have you chosen blow-by oxygen for this patient?

c. He is probably frightened and will tolerate oxygen near him, but not a mask directly placed on his face.

Rationale: Because any illness or traumatic event can be stressful and frightening to a child, blow-by oxygen is the best way to deliver a high concentration of oxygen to a child. It doesn't provide as high a concentration as a non-rebreather mask, but is very effective.

Question 199: The primary survey is used to:

d. Rapidly identify critical patients and life threatening conditions

Rationale: The primary survey is used to quickly identify any life threatening injuries or conditions that the patient may have. This includes your general impression of the patient, the patient's level of consciousness, the patient's chief complaint or obvious life threats, the quality of the patient's airway, breathing, and circulation, and a transport decision. All of the other answer choices happen either prior to the primary survey or after primary survey.

Question 200: While talking with a group of daycare children you notice a child who seems to be having an increased work of breathing. Which of the following signs helped you come to this decision?

a. Head bobbing

Rationale: When observing the childs respiratory effort, note any signs of increased work of breathing including: Accessory muscle use, retractions, head bobbing, nasal flaring, or tachypnea.

Question 201: Driving an ambulance fast?

b. Increases the stopping distance

Rationale: The faster you drive, the longer of a distance it will take for you to stop.

Question 202: You arrive on scene with your partner Dale to find a woman in respiratory distress. She is walking around with her hands up in the air and you can hear audible wheezing on inspiration. Bystanders tell you that she was eating a hot dog when she started choking. It has been 10 minutes since she started having breathing difficulties. The best course of action would be?

b. Transport and encourage her to cough

Rationale: Until there is a complete blockage of air you do not want to give the Heimlich maneuver. Best treatment in this situation would be to encourage the patient to cough and transport them to the hospital.

Question 203: An adult with a respiration rate of _____ per minute would be considered within normal limits. A child aged 3-5 with a respiration rate of _____ per minute would be considered within normal limits and an infant who is breathing at _____ per minute would be considered within normal limits.

d. 16, 25, 40

Rationale: According to NES guidelines normal adult respiratory rates are from 16-20 - preschool aged children (3-5) children are 20-30 and infants are 40-60 initially and drop to 30-40 after a few minutes.

Question 204: Your patient is a 75 year old male who may have had a stroke. He is unconscious and breathing with snoring respirations. After performing a head tilt chin lift maneuver, the snoring is still present. What is your best course of action?

c. Insert a nasopharyngeal, measured from the nostril to the earlobe

Rationale: The snoring is likely caused by the tongue falling back against the pharynx. The snoring may be eliminated by inserting a properly measured nasopharyngeal. If the head tilt did not help open the airway, the jaw thrust is even less likely to be effective. Snoring respirations are not usually caused by secretions in the mouth.

Question 205: You are dispatched to the call of a woman with a severe stomach ache. When you arrive on scene you find her doubled over in pain lying on the floor of the bathroom. There is vomit in the toilet and your patient is complaining that she is going to vomit again. She denies falling or having any pain anywhere but her stomach. Assessing her abdomen you find it to be very tender to the touch and she pulls away when you palpate only 1/2 inch deep. What other signs and symptoms might you find with this patient?

a. Tachycardia - hypotension - fever

Rationale: The patient is not likely to have crepitus, having no pain and denying that they fell, a person with broken ribs is unlikely to be breathing fast and deep, and if a person has been vomiting copius amounts it is likely they would be in metabolic alkalosis rather than acidosis.

Question 206: You and your partner Duval arrive on scene to find a woman who has suffered a blunt trauma to the chest from a swing on a carnival ride. She is having difficulty breathing and upon auscultation you hear nothing on the right side. This woman likely has a _____ and would be suffering from _____ as the collapsed lung is incapable of oxygenating any blood.

b. Pneumothorax / hypoxia

Rationale: No breath sounds on one side is characteristic of a pneumothorax or collapsed lung. This condition would make oxygenation of the blood difficult at half capacity and cause the patient to be hypoxic.

Question 207: You and your partner Sue have just arrived on scene to an unknown injury/ illness. You see a man lying against the side of a convenience store who appears unconscious. One of the witnesses tells you that the man was standing there and then just fell over hitting his head on the building and sliding down into the sitting position. As you check his pulse and respirations you find that he is breathing shallow at about 10 per minute, and his pulse is rapid. What would you do first for this patient?

d. Maintain c spine and move him to a supine position, then open his airway

Rationale: Knowing that he did fall you should take c spine precautions and get the airway open ASAP.

Question 208: Respirations in an adolescent would be considered normal at _____.

a. 16 breaths per minute

Rationale: According to the NES (National Education Standards) adolescence (13-18 years) begins at the onset of puberty until adulthood. The respiratory rate for this age group is 12-20 per minute.

Question 209: You arrive on scene with your partner Emilio to find a woman who is having problems breathing. She is speaking in 1 or 2 word bursts and is on oxygen at 3 liters per minute. There is an ashtray next to her bed loaded with cigarette butts. She says her care taker called the ambulance and she does not want you there. She says she will allow you to take her vitals but then you have to leave. Her BP is 100/60 her pulse is 48 and her respirations are 18. She says she is 89 years old and has a pacemaker and is on high blood pressure medication. "I just want to be old, please leave", she says. What should you do?

c. Respect her wishes and leave, asking her to please call if she needs medical attention

Rationale: As long as the patient is of sound mind you must respect their request to be left alone. Reminding her that you are a phone call away is not a bad idea.

Question 210: Which of the following would be a sign that CPR may not be necessary?

a. Stiff neck and jaw

Rationale: A stiff neck and jaw may be a sign of rigor mortis and CPR would not be initiated if the patient were pulseless and apneic as well as having rigor mortis. Remember to assess for rigor mortis in at least 2 joints. The other answer choices would all be indications of a possible need to begin CPR.

Question 211: The heart muscle has the ability to contract without neural stimulation. This is called?

a. Automaticity

Rationale: Automaticity is the ability of the heart muscle to generate and utilize it's own electrical impulses to contract.

Question 212: You and your partner Ebstein have been summoned to a residence where a 53 yr old woman has had a syncopic episode. You arrive to find her sitting on the couch sipping a glass of water. She states that she is feeling perfectly fine now. At this time a teenage girl enters the room with a monster mask in her hand. She tells you that she frightened her mother while wearing the mask. After administering oxygen to this patient, what would be the best course of action?_____What was most likely the cause of this woman's hypoperfusion?_____

c. Do a rapid trauma assessment to make sure she was not injured in the fall. Her sympathetic nervous system caused widespread vasodilation

Rationale: The woman is most likely fine and recovering from a case of psychogenic shock resulting from her daughter's prank. Lying supine for a short time is often all that is necessary to treat this condition. Doing a rapid trauma assessment would be appropriate in order to verify she was not hurt in the fall. The fainting spell is caused by the sympathic response to the scare. Blood is shunted from the lower priority organs and there is widespread vasodilation resulting in the hypoperfusion to the brain.

Question 213: You are responding to the scene of a two car collision which will require you to drive on the state highway for approximately 10 miles and then exit on the right side where you will drive an additonal 1.5 miles to the scene. Which of the following answer choices would be the most proper way of doing this?

b. Before you enter the highway turn off your lights and sirens. Move to the far left or "passing lane" and then turn lights and sirens back on. As you approach the exit turn lights and sirens off again and move to the off ramp. Once on the off ramp turn lights and sirens back on.

Rationale: You should shut down your lights and sirens before entering the highway until you can get into the far left or "passing lane". Using the far left or "passing lane" should help you move faster through traffic. Shutting down lights and sirens will help reduce the chances of confusing other drivers which may cause them to do something unexpectedly. The same process should be used when exiting the highway. Shut off the lights and sirens and move to the right lane and then the exit ramp. Once off the highway you should engage the sirens and lights again

Question 214: Asthma is classified into two types.

b. Extrinsic asthma, which is more common in childhood, causes brochioles constriction as a result of an outside substance like dust. Intrinsic asthma is more common in adults where no specific cause for the bronchioles constriction can be identified

Rationale: Extrinsic is caused by an external source. Allergens, drugs, chemicals, pollution ect. Intrinsic has unknown causes and is usually associated with adults rather than children. No particular substance can be identified as the trigger.

Question 215: You and your partner Benji are called to an apartment complex for an 82 year old woman experiencing chest pain. You recognize the address as one that you have been to several times in the past few months. You enter the apartment to find the woman pale and diaphoretic. She has a BP of 198/99 and she is breathing at 20 breaths per minute. Which part of your assessment will determine her treatment?

b. OPQRST and SAMPLE

Rationale: In her assessment, the OPQRST and SAMPLE are what is needed to assess her. Oxygen and transport are treatments, not assessment. Age, sex, and allergies are down the list of needed information in the assessment.

Question 216: The pediatric assessment triangle is composed of three elements:

c. Circulation, Appearance, Work of Breathing

Rationale: PAT is Work of Breathing, Skin Circulation, Appearance. The pediatric assessment triangle is used to form a rapid general impression of a child without making physical contact. Look at the child's appearance and muscle tone. Look at the work of breathing for signs of respiratory distress. Tachypnea or retractions of sternum and or intercostal muscles is a sign of respiratory difficulty. Look at the skin as a quick reference for circulation. Pallor can be a sign of poor circulation.

Question 217: Which of the following would be considered a priority patient?

c. A 55 year old female who has a blood pressure of 178/90

Rationale: A blood pressure of 178/90 would be a hypertensive crisis and would be considered a priority patient. The other patients 'could' turn into priority patients if their condition indicated so, but from the information given in the question they are not the highest priority patient.

Question 218: You and your partner Bob are just pulling up to a call for a man down with CPR in progress. Dispatch has told you that the man has an extensive cardiac history and had just finished golfing with friends when he collapsed in the parking lot. According to the AHA which of the sequences is most correct?

c. BSI, Check pulse, Begin compressions, Open airway

Rationale: 2010 guidelines use CAB- Chest Compressions, Airway, and Breathing. 2005 guidelines used ABC. This is the biggest change in the new guidelines. 2010 guidelines recommend to immediately begin compressions rather than opening the patient's airway and beginning ventilations as in the 2005 guidelines. Rescuers should recognize agonal gasps/ineffective breathing, and unresponsiveness as signs of cardiac arrest, but begin CPR with compressions. An AED should be used as soon as possible when the rescuer has witnessed the arrest.

Question 219: What is dependant lividity?

c. Blood settling at the lowest point in the body and visible through the skin

Rationale: A patient may show signs of blood pooling and skin discolorization after being in the same position for an extended period of time. This can be an indication of death.

Question 220: You arrive on scene to find a 101 year old woman who is sitting in a wheelchair smoking a cigarette. Her eyes are closed but she opens them when she hears you come into the room. You ask her name, she seems confused. You ask her to reach out and grab your hand, she does without hesitation. This woman has a GCS of what?

c. 14

Rationale: She gets a 4 for opening her eyes spontaneously, a 6 for obeying command of reaching for hand, and a 4 because her verbal response was confused. That's 14.

Question 221: The patient is a 6 year old girl whose mother says has been sick for a few days and then started having breathing problems this morning. Upon assessment, you notice the child is flaring her nostrils and has a hoarse voice when talking. What is she most likely suffering from and what should you do?

c. She could have epiglottitis and needs to be transported with high flow O2 on an NRB

Rationale: Epiglottitis is known to strike children in this age group. Croup is usually in younger children. Transporting with airway support is the best answer.

Question 222: Your patient is an unresponsive 44 year old female who has a pulse but is not breathing. How should you proceed with CPR?

b. 2 quick rescue breaths and then provide 10-12 breaths per minute

Rationale: AHA guidelines state that If she has a pulse, you only want to provide ventilatory support with 2 rescue breaths and 10-12 breaths per minute.

Question 223: What should be done to a French tip catheter after suctioning a patient's airway?

b. Flush with sterile water in preparation for additional suctioning

Rationale: Anticipating the need for additional suctioning should be followed by cleansing of the catheter with sterile water.

Question 224: You assess a young man who has yellow colored sclera. You would suspect he is suffering from?

d. Liver failure

Rationale: Liver problems often manifest themselves as a yellowing of the sclera. As seen with jaundice.

Question 225: What is a primary cause of abdominal pain and tenderness upon palpation?

c. Rupture of the gastrointestinal tract

Rationale: A rupture of any part of the gastrointestinal tract is the primary cause of most infected peritonitis patients. This can be assessed by eliciting the Blumberg sign or Rebound Tenderness. Blood in the retroperitoneal space would probably present as back pain, not abdominal pain. The irritation of the pericardium would cause chest pain, and if there is fecal leakage in the pleural space of your patient they have been in some serious trauma. The pleural space is between the linings of the lungs and isn't in direct contact with the abdominal cavity or it's organs.

Question 226: During anaphylactic shock, the patient's BP is likely to _____.

b. Decrease

Rationale: Anaphylaxis will likely produce a low blood pressure as the vasculature is dilated. This dilation can increase chances of shock as well.

Question 227: There are two separate respiratory drives. The _____ and the
_____. If a COPD patient is a carbon dioxide retainer then_____

a. Hypoxic / Carbon dioxide / You should deliver oxygen via nasal canula at 4-6 LPM

Rationale: Hypoxic drive stimulates the breathing centers in the brain when the oxygen levels in the blood drop too low. It is secondary to Carbon dioxide drive which stimulates the brain's breathing centers when the levels of carbon dioxide in the blood get too high.

Question 228: Who decides what the minimum data set is for a PCR?

c. NEMSES

Rationale: National Education Standards lists the minimum data set for PCRs

Question 229: You are treating a patient who is complaining of chest pain. They are diaphoretic with a blood pressure of 98/50. You have their medications on board which include a prescription for nitroglycerin. Medical control has instructed you to administer 1 nitroglycerin tablet sublingually. How would you respond?

d. Repeat the vital signs to medical control and ask if they still wish to have you administer the nitroglycerin with the blood pressure that low.

Rationale: Administering nitroglycerin is contraindicated in patients with a blood pressure of less than 100 (Systolic), however it is always the best option to repeat the information to medical control if they give an order you think might be dangerous. Many doctors would have no problem with administering nitroglycerin to a patient who has a borderline BP, but you want to make sure they understand your concern. Ultimately you are an extension of the medical direction and unless you are sure the prescribed treatment will cause harm, you should follow the directions after clarifying the information. You should never blindly follow orders however. You need to make informed and educated treatment decisions.

Question 230: A 5 year old boy has fallen down the stairs at a daycare. You have responded with your partner Oli. Utilizing the PAT, what would you use to rapidly form a general impression of this patient?

a. Your eyes and ears

Rationale: The PAT uses only the eyes and ears to form a general impression of the patient. Looking at the child's appearance and muscle tone, Determining how the child is breathing, and looking at the condition of the skin with regards to circulation, is all that is required.

Question 231: 911 dispatch calls you to the scene of a "man down". You arrive to find a man sitting up against the wall of his garage. He has a glazed look in his eyes and abnormal respirations. The breaths begin slow and shallow and then gradually get faster and deeper. The rate and depth then decrease to the point of apnea. What do you suspect is wrong with this patient? What are you going to do for them?

d. They had a stroke / Give high flow oxygen

Rationale: Cheyne-Stokes is the name associated with the breathing pattern in this question. It is most often associated with stroke and metabolic problems. Periods of apnea and or irregular breaths can also point to stroke. The obvious first intervention for this patient is to administer oxygen.

Question 232: Dispatch has called your unit to an MVA involving a city bus and a minivan. The driver of the minivan plowed into the side of the bus as it was stopping to pick up passengers. Everyone on the bus is fine, but the driver of the minivan is having difficulty breathing. His pulse rate is very rapid and his jugular veins are bulging. His trachea has shifted from the midline and his skin is cool and pale. He is complaining of severe chest pain and has a bottle of nitro clutched in his hand. What is likely wrong with this man, and what is considered proper treatment?

b. This man likely has a tension pneumothorax caused by impact to the steering wheel. Treatment would include performing a needle thoracentesis

Rationale: All signs point to a pneumo or hemopneumothorax. Answer 1, while he may have had a heart attack, the signs say otherwise. You would not likely be administering nitro to this patient. Answer 3, A dissected aorta is a possibility from the collision, but will not cause tracheal deviation nor distended jugular veins. Answer 4, although this man could have a pleural effusion from the collision, administering a diuretic in the prehospital setting is not appropriate treatment.

Question 233: You arrive on scene with your partner to a restaurant where a man was reported to be choking. You enter and find an unconscious cyanotic male on the floor. He is supine with BBQ sauce on his mouth and a napkin in his hand. What would you do for this patient?

d. Head tilt, chin lift, verify apnea and begin Compressions. Upon completion of the compressions, give two slow breaths looking for chest rise and fall.

Rationale: Open the airway and check to see if they are breathing, if not, begin compressions first. After completing the initial set of compressions, give two slow breaths looking for chest rise and fall. Continue this sequence until the object has been removed.

Question 234: Cheyne-Stokes breathing is characterized by _____.

a. Uneven breaths with periods of apnea

Rationale: Cheyne-Stokes is often seen in head injuries and is characterized by uneven or progressive breaths with periods of apnea.

Question 235: You have an unconscious patient. What do you do?

c. ABCs, History taking, Rapid full body scan

Rationale: According to the NES, the ABCs are part of the primary survey, which is then followed by history taking, and then the secondary assessment. A rapid full body scan is the first step of the secondary assessment. The rapid full body scan may be incorporated into the primary survey in order to determine life threats. You would not start CPR as the patient is only unconscious. They may be breathing with a pulse. Baseline vitals come after the primary and secondary assessments. Transport decision also comes before vital signs.

Question 236: The Incident Command System (ICS) is used to:

a. Ensure efficient use of resources, public and responder safety as well as the successful completion of incident management goals.

Rationale: The primary focus of the Incident Command System is to establish a well organized, safe, efficiently managed inciden scene. It can be used on a simple call involving only 1 responding unit or a call the uses hundreds of resources and involves multiple agencies.

Question 237: You and your partner Toby arrive at a motel in response to a 911 call for an unconscious female. You find the woman pulseless and while Toby hooks up the AED, you begin delivering compressions. How many compressions per minute would you give this woman?

b. 100-109 compressions per minute

Rationale: 100-109 compressions per minute would satisfy AHA CPR Guidelines which state that AT LEAST 100 compressions per minute should be delivered.

Question 238: You arrive on scene with your partner Aaron to a call of an unknown injury/ illness. You pull into the driveway of an apartment building. In the parking area is a woman lying face up with her eyes closed. After making sure the scene is safe, what would be the most efficient means for gathering useful information on this patient?

b. Check her pulse with your hand while you put your ear near her mouth and look down the sternum for chest rise

Rationale: You need to determine her level of responsiveness, assess her pulse, and see whether she is breathing or not. This should be best achieved with the 2nd answer.

Question 239: Incident Command has put you in charge of setting up the landing zone for a helicopter transport. What size area will you try to procure for this zone? What is the minimum acceptable size for this zone?

b. 100 feet X 100 feet / minimum of 60 feet X 60 feet

Rationale: 100 feet by 100 feet square is the preferred size of a helicopter landing zone at night. It should not be smaller than 60 feet by 60 feet during the day.

Question 240: A child is breathing at 32 breaths per minute. This would be considered _____.

b. Above range

Rationale: Child respiration rates should be between 20 and 30.

Question 241: Chest compressions on a newborn that is not breathing adequately should be done at what depth?

b. about 1/3 to 1/2 the depth of the chest

Rationale: About 1/3 to 1/2 the depth of the chest with both thumbs. Hands should be wrapped around the thorax.

Question 242: A 4 year old boy has fallen from a swing and landed on his side. He is complaining of stomach pain. Which of the following assessment techniques would not be utilized to determine if this child is going into shock?

d. Taking his blood pressure

Rationale: A low blood pressure is most often associated with decompensated shock and is a late, ominous sign in children who are sick or injured. Taking a blood pressure would not be used to determine if the child is going into shock.

Question 243: A freight car has overturned and is spilling hundreds of gallons of hazardous chemicals into a local creek. Incident Command has told you that the toxicity of the hazardous material is a level 3. What level of protection must any personnel entering this area be wearing?

d. Level A or B protection

Rationale: Toxicity level 3 is very hazardous and thus requires a high level of protection. Level A or B protection is required in this case. Toxicity goes from 0 to 4, with 4 being the worst and 0 being little or no threat. Protection level goes from A to D. A being the highest level of protection and D being the lowest level of protection.

Question 244: You and your partner Obi have been dispatched to a home for breathing difficulties. You arrive to find a 50 year old man in bed with labored breathing. His respiration rate is 20 with only very slight chest rise. His color is slightly pale and his pulse is weak. Family members tell you that the man has AIDS. When this history is presented Obi says, " I am sorry, but I don't want to catch AIDS. I can't help". Obi then leaves the house. What has just occurred?

a. Obi has abandoned the patient by refusing to administer care. He has a duty to act

Rationale: Denying care to this patient would be considered abandonment, even if Obi believed the man posed an infectious risk. His action can also be a violation of the Americans with Disabilities Act and possibly constitute negligence if the other 4 base criteria are met. There was no breakdown in communication from his statement. The family and patient may not be happy about Obi's statement, but it is a stretch to say that he has compromised the family and patient's trust in EMS. It is also not likely that you could determine on scene, that the family has suffered psychological damage as a result of the statement.

Question 245: You and your partner Nick are dispatched to the scene of a small building fire, just as backup and possible rehabilitation. As you round a corner near the scene, you see 10-12 people lying in a yard a few houses away from the fire. Some are in obvious distress and others are walking aimlessly down the street.. Which of the following choices would be the most appropriate for you and Nick to take?

d. Contact the IC and notify them of the current situation, triage and order more resources through command

Rationale: Getting additional help on the way to treat multiple patients is the best choice of action.

Question 246: You have just arrived on scene to a call of man down. A man is lying prone on the sidewalk outside of a bar and there are several bystanders who say they witnessed him just fall over forward. As you check his pulse and respirations you find that he is breathing shallow at about 8 per minute and his pulse is 112. What would be the proper choice of action?

b. While maintaining c-spine precautions log roll him to a supine position and open his airway

Rationale: Knowing that he did fall you should take c-spine precautions and get the airway open ASAP. Shaking the patient may exacerbate any unknown injury.

Question 247: You arrive on scene at a local park for a reported drug overdose. A man in his 30's, pale, with an obvious altered LOC comes stumbling toward you and your partner. He mumbles something unintelligible and then lies down in front of you in a supine position. His respirations are of normal depth, but the rate is a little bit fast. He has a fixed gaze, straight up, and he continues mumbling something about "His sister and a hamburger". A quick check of his pulse reveals he is tachycardic and you note his skin is moist. A blood pressure reading shows 138/82. What is most likely wrong with this man and what would be the most appropriate course of treatment?

b. He is hypoglycemic and has diabetes mellitus. The most appropriate treatment would include checking his blood sugar level, putting him on high flow O2 via NRB, and administering glucose if necessary

Rationale: Some signs of hypoglycemia include altered LOC, diaphoresis, normal or rapid breathing and pulse, and extreme hunger. Answer one, while possible, would definitely not be appropriate to suction this patient as there is no airway obstruction. Answer 2 is not likely, as hyperglycemia will cause the skin to be warm and or dry not moist, and blood pressure will more likely be low during hyperglycemia as a result of the dehydration. Answer 4.....wow. While the "ol' poison dart to the neck" is possible the treatment is not probable.

Question 248: Your patient is an 8 year old girl who fell from a swing and hit her head. She has a pulse but is not breathing. Your CPR should include what?

a. Breaths at a rate of 12-20

Rationale: AHA Guidelines specify that for all children, a rescue breath rate of 12-20 is to be used.

Question 249: A report of a woman with an acute abdominal complaint comes in on the ambulance radio. You and your partner Lebomowitz arrive to find a 45-year-old woman holding her stomach. You perform a primary survey and administer oxygen via NRB as Lebomowitz begins history taking. According to the NREMT medical assessment skill sheet, what should you do next?

d. Do a secondary assessment focusing on her chief complaint

Rationale: According to the NREMT you would follow history taking with a secondary assessment. In this case it would be focused on her chief complaint. This may be her stomach or something else. Don't get tunnel vision. Assessing airway, breathing, skin condition and pulse are part of the primary survey, which is followed by history taking not the secondary survey.

Question 250: A 26 year old woman has called the ambulance because she has begun delivery of her baby. Dispatch says the mother stated the baby's foot was sticking out of the vaginal opening. You should be prepared to?

b. Place patient into a knee to chest position and rapid transport

Rationale: Allow gravity to assist you in keeping the child in the canal until definitive care.

Made in the USA
San Bernardino, CA
05 April 2013